GOD
HAS
SPOKEN

By Gordon M. Hyde

Southern Publishing Association
Nashville, Tennessee

GOD
HAS
SPOKEN

Library of Congress Catalog Card No. 75-40913
SBN 8127-0109-7

This book was edited by Richard Coffen, designed by Dean Tucker.
Photography by Dave Damer. Type set 10/11 Times Roman.

Printed in U.S.A.

2—

CONTENTS

TESTING THE FOUNDATIONS

When one of the world's best-known English-language newsmagazines carries a Christmas cover story with the title "How True Is the Bible?"[1] we sense some indication of the remarkable way in which religious issues have been catapulted into the headlines of the news media in the past few years.

Perhaps it is significant that the *Time* story did not even mention Seventh-day Adventists. Or is it? Have we not taken it for granted that the Bible is true? And have we not been so busy carrying its Good News to the ends of the earth that we have felt no concern with the challenge brought by modern Biblical criticism and skeptical approaches to the Bible? Perhaps, in fact, we have something of a blind side toward "higher criticism." We know little and have even cared less about the rather subjective approach of the modern Biblical critic who claims to be so objective and so scientific that he cannot grant historical validity to the great miracles of divine intervention in human affairs as portrayed in Scripture.

Recently the news media have portrayed the Lutheran Church-Missouri Synod, a body of two and a half million traditionally conservative, Bible-believing Protestants, as in the throes of internal struggle and potential schism over the historical reality of such Biblical events as the Creation, the Flood, the Exodus, Jonah and the whale, the virgin birth, the miracles of Jesus, and His literal resurrection. Reportedly, the majority of the faculty at the LCMS Seminary—Concordia, in St. Louis, Missouri—have been gradually abandoning faith in such Biblical "events" and for some years have been sending "unbelieving" students into the denomination's pulpits.

[1]*Time,* December 30, 1974, pp. 34-41.

The internal LCMS controversy has made headlines in both the secular and the religious press.[2] And the question comes to mind: Can the Seventh-day Adventist Church take it for granted that it is immune from the possibility of a similar controversy within its ranks?

Although on the surface this book may seem to deal with the obvious and the basic, it seeks to reaffirm the divine authority of the Bible in our time. Scripture is God's chosen channel in which divine revelation and inspiration have made known God's character and His will for man and the universe, and Christianity is a revealed faith, not something man has created in his evolutionary development. *God Has Spoken* tries to give the positive (and hopefully simple) affirmations of the Bible and the Ellen G. White writings which provide a bulwark against that highly subjective, rationalizing, critical, and philosophical approach to Scripture which has eroded its full authority in many churches. With the resultant loss of their God-given mission, these churches have turned to other bases of mission—sociological, humanistic, psychological, rationalistic, or existential—rather than the Biblical.

So the thesis of this volume is that *God has spoken.* He has not been waiting to be "discovered" or "created" by an evolving man. And the Bible is not merely one of the highest achievements of man's spiritual urges. It is the word of the God who has chosen to seek out rebellious man and to speak to him—revealing Himself to him in word, in action, and by intervening in human history.

This evaluation of and attitude toward the Bible has undergirded the Seventh-day Adventist faith as well as the traditional faith of all historical Protestants. In such a time as ours, it is appropriate to borrow the words of David, spoken at the time of one of his great crises: "If the foundations be destroyed, what can the righteous do?" (Psalm 11:3).

Interestingly, even while wishing to remain somewhat within the circle of Biblical criticism, the writer of the *Time* cover story, referred to at the outset of this Introduction, closed the piece with an acknowl-

---

[2]Examples: *Time,* "Red Sea Heresy," April 3, 1972, p. 56; "Civil War in the Synod," September 25, 1972, p. 59; "Battle of New Orleans," July 23, 1973, p. 69; "Lutherans at War," September 9, 1974, p. 66. *Newsweek,* "The Lutheran Pope," July 23, 1973, p. 50. *Christianity Today,* "The Battle of New Orleans," August 10, 1973, p. 40; "Integrity, Schism, Neither, Both," October 25, 1974, p. 11.

edgment that points in the direction the ensuing discussion will take: "Some time, some where, God intervened in history to help man. Whether it was at the time of the Exodus, the giving of the Law, the Incarnation or the Resurrection, or any of those many smaller interventions that are still so cherished, ordinary human history was interrupted, and has never since been the same."

CHAPTER I

THE SELF-REVEALING GOD

People like to figure things out. We call the process reasoning and the result philosophy—our way of trying to understand the universe and ourselves. Over the centuries the big, basic questions have not changed much, and neither have our human answers. However, at various times and by various means, God has intervened to ask some of His questions and to provide some of His answers. And His questions more than cover ours (see Hebrews 1:1-3).

When people want to be independent (by assuming, for example, that they are the crowning result of a self-originating and self-perpetuating process of evolution), they are less likely to be interested in and susceptible to the questions and answers offered by God. In fact, they tend to make up their own ideas about "god," even if they do not shape "him" out of wood or stone.

Now we do not find many happy alternatives in this situation. If our God is indeed God, He is neither the discovery nor the invention of human beings. Neither can any other "gods" be truly God. He who is indeed God is above and beyond and before and after all animate and inanimate things. As Source and Sustainer, He alone initiates and makes possible any conversation and any communication. In His Word, which we assume to be the Bible, He asserts again and again that He is the self-revealing God. "In the beginning God . . ." (Genesis 1:1). "He which testifieth these things saith . . ." (Revelation 22:20). Francis A. Schaeffer has written effectively, "He is there and He is not silent" (*The God Who Is There,* Tyndale House Publishers, Wheaton, Illinois, 1972).

Is it surprising, therefore, that John portrays Christ, the Second Person of the Godhead, as the *Logos,* the Word? Knowing seems to demand language, and Jesus, the divine *Logos,* is the Bible's answer to our knowing. God is there, and He is speaking to all His moral creatures. "When all things began, the Word already was. The Word dwelt with God, and what God was, the Word was. The Word, then, was with God at the beginning, and through him all things came to be; no single thing was created without him" (John 1:1-3, NEB*).

Can we think of a self-revealing God (or being or entity) who would be impersonal? If all that *is* began with the impersonal, what meaning would there be in the universe for us? How could we fit in and relate? Perhaps this has something to do with the spreading meaninglessness of life for our contemporaries, because many no longer believe in a personal God.

And can we think of a person existing before the beginning of the universe who would not also be infinite? Could there be anything or anyone *before* God who would not then Himself be the true God? So, as demanded by the situation, the self-revealing God of the Bible portrays Himself as infinite. "Through him all things came to be; no single thing was created without him" (John 1:3, NEB).

So far as we have gone, then, God provides the answers to all these big questions. But there is another. Could it be that God *needed* to create people, or other moral creatures, in order to have someone to love? No, God did not *need* such. The philosophical question of unity and diversity finds its answer in God the Father, God the Son, and God the Holy Spirit. What a revelation—an infinite, personal unity and diversity in God!

As Schaeffer observes, no other philosophy or religion can provide such answers to the whole world's greatest and basic questions. However, the God of the Bible—the self-revealing, infinite, personal God with the unity and diversity of the Trinity—is that answer. How infinitely grateful and unapologetic we should be for this revelation! Surely it is time to present the self-revealing God to the twentieth century in terms which show that the God of the Bible is the answer to the questions we are asking, yet cannot answer on our own.

The question also arises as to why God should desire to create mankind and to initiate communication. God lacked nothing; He did

---

*From the New English Bible. Copyright, The Delegates of the Oxford University Press and The Syndics of the Cambridge University Press, 1961, 1970. Reprinted by permission.

not decide, "I'm lonely; I'll make Me a man." The creation of our race with all its privileges, hazards, and high destiny can be seen (and then but faintly understood) only in the light of God's constant willingness to share, to give of Himself, and to minister to the happiness of others at infinite and unfathomable risk to Himself. God wanted us as His daughters and sons to reflect His likeness, for He made us in His image.

Then, too, perhaps our recognition that God has revealed Himself is significant not only for what that recognition tells us about ourselves, but also for what it tells about God. In our pride of intellect and independence we would like to centralize ourselves in our knowledge of God and to portray Him as the extension of ourselves or as the reflection of our own image. But the self-revealing God will never lend His support to such subterfuge.

According to the psalmist, God is great, greatly to be praised, and his greatness is *unsearchable*. If these words are true, then God is not the creation of human minds—not even the most pious and spiritual of them. No matter how skillfully we press our research, nor how logical and consistent our reasoning, God transcends all human thought and knowledge. "His greatness is unsearchable" (Psalm 145:3). And for any who at times feel apprehensive of eternity or fear the possibility of eventual unending boredom, David's words can offer assurance. Should the privileged inhabiter of eternity probe every microorganism and search the infinitudes of illimitable space, God will ever challenge his mind because of His own eternal greatness.

Yet, when humble men with little literary or scientific training asked Jesus Christ to show them God, He gave them an answer as overwhelming in its simplicity as in its depth. "He who has seen me has seen the Father" (John 14:9, RSV). The unsearchably great God is like Jesus Christ in His character, but Jesus' humanity shrouded that infinite greatness in much the same way that the sanctuary in the midst of Israel veiled the Shekinah of Yahweh.

Christ mercifully veiled His glory for the same reason that Moses, at Israel's insistence, veiled his face when it shone with the reflected glory of his meeting with Yahweh in the mountaintop (see Exodus 34:29-35). Yet the God-man, Jesus Christ, the Righteous One, reveals all that we now need to know of the unsearchable God (see Chapter 5). We can only conclude that God *must* reveal Himself to us if we are to know Him and *must* love us infinitely to send His Son so that we might know Him and His saving purposes.

Speaking of the self-revealing God, does it ever occur to us that only God Himself *could* perfectly reveal God to us? How could any finite one adequately reveal the Infinite, the created reveal the Uncreated, the loved reveal Him who personifies love? Do we often think of His condescension in reaching down to our rebellious race in order to reveal Himself? Do we sense that through this self-revelation we, coming to know Him as the Source of love, may have another opportunity to love Him as we should have in the beginning?

It seems also that we all have some kind of expectation of the Infinite One. We have our human heroes and heroines, our ideals. Could God be anything other than infinitely more wise and noble than the wisest and noblest of our race? Or is the God of Scripture only a shade above our human best? Could He be the creation of the spiritually sensitive Bible authors whose writings must not be taken literally, for they have merely given us one of the highest concepts of "God" to date (along with other great spiritual minds from the non-Christian world)? Or let's put it another and opposite way: Could anyone suggest the characteristics of a God who would be more worthy of Godhood than the God of the entire Bible? Does He not live up to all our expectations of God?

We stress here the immeasurable gap between God and His creatures—even though He has created us in His own image—because our pride has blurred our view of that gulf. As modern scientific people, we think ourselves self-sufficient and independent—certainly not God-dependent. It is not surprising, then, to find us without sharp distinctions in our thinking between the natural and the supernatural, between the human and the divine, between the temporal and the eternal. And the absence of these distinctions robs God of His transcendence, if not His very existence. Remember the "God is dead" wave of half a dozen years ago? It logically and consistently followed the steady erosion of our recognition of God's transcendence.

The modern view of God is a far cry from that seen by the prophets of ancient times. In their visions of God or in their meetings with the Angel of God's presence, they keenly, abjectly, felt the infinite gulf between God and His creatures. Sensing their unworthiness to be in

His presence, they consistently prostrated themselves before Him or His messengers.

Seventh-day Adventists have urgent reason to keep in tune with the prophetic view of God. The three angels of Revelation 14 call us to worship the kind of God the prophets met. And that same God is coming to reign eternally over the redeemed kingdom of His creating. If Seventh-day Adventists lose their clear view of the transcendent God, can they escape the condition of those Christian churches that have lost their sense of His reality, greatness, power, and righteousness?

When we minimize God's transcendence and maximize His immanence or closeness to us, it is not a long step to pantheism. In pantheism God is everything and everything is God. It obliterates God's personality by deifying all laws, forces, and objects of the universe. Seventh-day Adventists should, from their earlier history, have a built-in immunity to and alertness against pantheism in any form. We have had one major battle over that already, and we cannot progress by fighting that one again!

At the same time, our love and adoration of God as well as our own renewal in the divine image is proportional to our view of God's transcendent exaltation. "If it were possible for us to attain to a full understanding of God and His word, there would be no further discovery of truth, no greater knowledge, no further development. God would cease to be supreme, and man would cease to advance. Thank God, it is not so" (*Education,* p. 172).

But, thank God, the transcendent God is not the distant, indifferent God of the deist. He has not set machinery in operation only to forget that He made it. The transcendent God is the acting, working, sustaining, self-sacrificing God. He will ultimately review before the assembled peoples of all ages His "marvels," such as had not been done in all the earth, nor in any nation (see Exodus 34:10). Although some of these acts seem awesome and terrible, some meant the provision of food and water for a widow and her son, or even concern for an injured sparrow.

In the school of the hereafter, with divine teachers and an eternity of opportunity, the redeemed will study "the course of the great conflict that had its birth before time began and that ends only when time shall cease. The history of the inception of sin; of fatal falsehood in its crooked working; of truth that, swerving not from its own straight lines, has met and conquered error—all will be made manifest. The veil that interposes between the visible and the invisible world will be drawn aside, and wonderful things will be revealed" (*ibid.*, p. 304).

But there will be no opportunity to enroll in the school of the hereafter for any who fail to reach out after the saving knowledge God offers now. Eternal life depends on a living, personal knowledge of and relationship with Jesus Christ—the One sent from God, yet who is also God (see John 17:3).

Obviously, it is more than theoretical knowledge that brings life eternal, or fallen Lucifer's great intellect would assure him of salvation. Some who had highly significant contact with Jesus on earth gained no salvation from the opportunity. Think of some of them —Judas, the rich young ruler, Herod, Pilate, Caiaphas, the people of Christ's hometown, and many of the "daughters of Jerusalem" who wept as Christ stumbled toward Golgotha.

It is a solemnizing thought that we may have grown up in or have been welcomed into the circle of Jesus' followers today and yet fail to enter eternal life. No casual contact with Jesus Christ will do. Jesus used a vine and its branches to illustrate the intimacy and permanence of the life-giving relationship. Where does the vine end? Where does the branch begin? Fiber by fiber and vein by vein the life of the vine becomes the life of the branch. The vine is in the branch. The branch is in the vine. Through such a union, we become living, fruitful branches of the "true vine" (see John 15:1-12).

So we have our introductory picture of the self-revealing God. We shall subsequently look into certain aspects in greater depth. But at this early stage we must answer the question, Who or what are the channels of God's self-revelation?

CHAPTER II

CHANNELS OF GOD'S SELF-REVELATION

Having asserted that God must choose to reveal Himself for us to know Him (since it does not lie in our power to discover Him), we want to assert our awareness of the human element in the communication process. *Communication* implies a receiver as well as a sender and also some channel through which the message flows from source to receiver.

In standard human communication, the channels mostly involve sound waves, light waves, and radio waves. More intimate communication involves the senses. But what channels would God use to communicate Himself to us?

We sense, of course, that sin has introduced some problems into the communication process, for if sin makes us God's enemies, we have some very special barriers to effective communication. And if God's unveiled presence will destroy anything contaminated by sin, then the presentation of His person to us would be as calamitous as His perpetual silence. Since God has spoken, however, what channels has He chosen?

God's two most vital channels—the Living Word (the *Logos*) and the Written Word (the Bible)—have some fascinatingly parallel characteristics. In each, the human veils the divine. Christ clothed His divinity with humanity so that He might come close to us without destroying us and so that He might be one with us and meet the enemy where we have to meet him. Similarly, the Bible is couched in human language so that God's thoughts and purposes might be expressed in code and come to us through channels appropriate to our comprehension. In some respects incarnation and revelation-inspiration have much in common.

Having said this, though, we have really not explained much.

Both main channels of God's communication embrace many mysterious elements, and there is little hope (or necessity) that we shall have the elements of mystery removed this side of eternity. Even if we admit this, it does nothing to detract from the effectiveness of the channels or the messages conveyed by them. When God works, we find some things mysterious to us—and gladly so, for we should not wish our God to be held to our limitations!

The perceptive reader is perhaps wondering how the incarnate Christ constitutes a channel of God's communication to us. He is not living on the earth in our day, neither were we in His. What do we *really* know about Him, and by what means? In reply we might point to the few minor mentions of His name recorded by historians of His age, but the references are slight. How then do we know what we know? Simply by the Bible—the Old Testament in prediction of His coming and the New in recording His coming—which brings us to the Bible, God's other main channel of communication. The Bible holds immeasurable significance.

If you find it difficult to keep the message and the channels separate, do not be much concerned. The various elements of the communication process are so intricately interwoven that we can scarcely do more than separate them in theory—very little in practice. The Bible is ink on paper. Light waves convey the awareness of the code to the eyes of the reader. But how important are those facts when compared with the meaning conveyed by the words to the reader's mind? Christ came here as the God-man, the "express image" of His Father. People heard Him, saw Him, touched Him, but what is that to the revelation He gave them in word and action of God's nature and character!

Some people focus on the limitations imposed by the human elements in these channels of God's communication. They seem to believe that human limitations make the divine unreal, or at least unreliable. It seems not to occur to them that the infinite God could transform, transfuse, and transfigure the human with the divine so that the result would be the Word of God. Many saw only a man when they saw Christ—His travel-stained peasant garments, His motley fisherman followers, His obvious poverty and humble birth. So also many see only an ancient collection of religious writings in the Bible. If Christ were *only* a man and the Bible *only* an ancient book, then there is no authority in either, nor any salvation. But the Biblical writers unequivocally claimed to have received a revelation from or by God.

By stressing the two major channels of God's communication, we did not intend to downplay or ignore the significance of the others. For some, the visible things of God—the universe in all its variety, unity, and essential harmony—reveal the invisible. The apostle Paul even intimates that the message of the invisible God from the visible will leave people without excuse for ignoring God's creative power and thus His "eternal power and Godhead" (see Romans 1:20).

It seems tragic that, in an age when human inventive genius has opened up the microworld of things too small for our unaided sight and the macroworld of illimitable space, many scientists should account for all these marvels by the processes of chance aided by unimaginable periods of time. Would we rather worship time itself than a personal, infinite, yet communicating God? Time will never explain the emergence of something from nothing—an unspoken presupposition of evolution.

"The material world is under God's control. The laws that govern all nature are obeyed by nature. Everything speaks and acts the will of the Creator. The clouds, the rain, the dew, the sunshine, the showers, the wind, the storm, all are under the supervision of God, and yield implicit obedience to Him who employs them. The tiny spear of grass bursts its way through the earth, first the blade, then the ear, and then the full corn in the ear. The Lord uses these, His obedient servants, to do His will. The fruit is first seen in the bud, enclosing the future pear, peach, or apple, and the Lord develops these in their proper season, because they do not resist His working. They do not oppose the order of His arrangements. His works, as seen in the natural world, are not one half comprehended or appreciated. These silent preachers will teach human beings their lessons, if they will only be attentive hearers" (Ellen G. White Comments, *SDA Bible Commentary,* Vol. 6, pp. 1067, 1068).

Not only natural history becomes a channel of God's communication, but human history does also. Although the scientific world might choose to include human history within natural history, for the Bible and for us, man and woman were the crowning work of God's creation and thoroughly distinct from all other creatures. For them and their descendants God has performed His great and mighty acts: the miracle of the Flood, destroying yet preserving; the multiple miracles in the call of Abram, the development and preservation of his lineage; the extensive miracles of the Exodus, extensive because of the numbers of people involved; the checkered career of Israel after Moses, but the hand of God ever ready to intervene to preserve the chosen people whom He had selected as channels of His self-revelation; the captivity and restoration of Israel; and the coming of the Redeemer of Israel and the Gentile world.

And that brings us back full circle to the supreme channel of God's revelation, Jesus Christ, the Living Word, the only flawless image of God. In fact, we find Jesus fully aware that He was the Sent of heaven and that His words and works revealed the Father-God: "For I have given unto them the words which thou gavest me; and they have received them, and have known surely that I came out from thee, and they have believed that thou didst send me" (John 17:8).

We will consider the revelation of God in Christ more fully in Chapter 5, but let us point out here that the supremacy and perfection of Jesus' revelation of God was directly proportionate to His self-effacement. We don't sense His material poverty, perhaps, because of His spiritual wealth, but the poorest of the poor would have been able to relate to Jesus. That is one key to the effectiveness of Christ as a channel of God's self-revelation.

From one point of view, it may be understandable that God's Son would serve as a channel of revelation. Various members of the British royal family represent Her Majesty at key functions. Even the Prince of Wales—he who may one day be the king in his own right—is her representative and channel of communication on occasion. But what does it tell us about God that He would condescend to use men—the children of the first human rebels against God's love—as His channels?

Have we been thrilled by the—may I say it?—audacity of God's plan to reveal Himself through the immediate followers of the Man who was nailed to the cross? How utterly different from sinful man God is! "I want you to wait in Jerusalem [Lord, surely not Jerusalem!] until you receive My power, and then I want you to witness to the multitudes that will be here from all over the world for the Feast of Pentecost." And we know the results. Men declared that they turned the world upside down! (Acts 17:6).

Modern theologians often discuss the process by which God's revelation through men came into the present written form. After studying German folklore, some assumed that the Bible also first existed in loose, oral traditions which eventually became standardized by repetition and the tests of time. Gradually it was committed to writing, and ultimately later writers arranged, collated, and manipulated it to say, under the guise of ancient and divine authority, what was needed at the time. So the Biblical scholars spend much time sorting out the supposed layers of tradition and determining who copied from whom.

We plan to comment more fully on this aspect in chapters 6 and 7, but for now let us simply assert that the God who is not silent has ensured the adequate transmission of His messages through human channels. Indeed, the Biblical writers (and also Ellen G. White) were aware of the significance of the writing aspect of their work. They felt the divine power assisting and directing in the writing so that the resultant message is marked with the authority of the words of God, although it utilizes the words of men.

God not only had His channels of communication anciently, He also has them today. Through them the Holy Spirit—"the Spirit of truth" (John 16:13)—chooses to reveal the truth about God to the church, and through the church to the world, until Christ comes in glory.

As soon as we mention the Holy Spirit and the church, we recall the gifts of the Spirit (Ephesians 4, Romans 12, and 1 Corinthians 12-14). Among them is the gift of prophecy, which Seventh-day Adventists believe has been particularly granted in the life and work of Ellen G. White. As we move ahead in this book, we will deal with these various aspects of the total means by which God has revealed Himself to mankind. First, however, we must go back to the beginning and look not only at the channels of revelation themselves, but also at the message, the authority, and the significance of those messages which He has sent.

First, God speaks by what He makes.

Chapter III

GOD SPEAKS BY WHAT HE MAKES

Perhaps the reader is a collector of shells, a scaler of the highest mountains, or a soaring glider who with machineless silence climbs the upsweeping invisible mountains of air. If the reader is a radiologist, a neurosurgeon, or a physiologist, then the daily confrontation with the mysteries of the human body will lead him or her and all other sensitive observers of nature to concede that God speaks by what He makes.

This chapter will concentrate upon the ways God's created works speak to us about Him and what they tell us. And we are immediately in the arena of theological and scientific controversy. Reduced to its simplest terms, the debate could take us back to the famous "monkey trials" in which two nonscientists (one a master of words and the other a master of debate) argued the rights and wrongs of requiring public schools to teach only creation as the theory of origins. (Isn't it fascinating to consider that in these seventies an Adventist doctor has led a battle in California to require that science textbooks in public schools mention creation as one of the options in a theory of origins?)

The Bible writers consistently present God as the Creator of the universe and suggest no alternative for its origin or maintenance. Jesus Himself spoke of the Genesis account as if it was authentic and factual (see Matthew 19:4; Mark 10:6). "Well," counters one, "if He had presented anything that revolutionary, no one would have listened to Him." Are we seriously suggesting that Jesus Christ presented nothing revolutionary? Why then did men crucify Him? But let us notice a specific here. If Christ had opened to His generation just little windows upon the factual truths of the universe, they might have missed the most vital aspect of God's revelation—His plan to save us from sin.

"Jesus is the Light that lighteth every man that cometh into the world. He is the Light of the world, and He bids us come unto Him, and learn of Him. Jesus was the great Teacher. He could have made disclosures on the sciences that would have placed the discoveries of the greatest men in the background as utter littleness; but this was not His mission or His work. He had come to seek and to save that which was lost, and He could not permit Himself to be turned from His one object. He allowed nothing to divert Him" (*Fundamentals of Christian Education,* p. 183).

"Christ might have opened to men the deepest truths of science. He might have unlocked mysteries that have required centuries of toil and study to penetrate. He might have made suggestions in scientific lines that would have afforded food for thought and stimulus for invention to the close of time. But He did not do this. He said nothing to gratify curiosity or to satisfy man's ambitions by opening doors to worldly greatness" (*Testimonies,* Vol. 8, p. 201).

Let us rest, with Jesus and the Holy Spirit who inspired the Bible writers, in the assurance that God indeed was and is the Creator and Sustainer. "He spake, and it was done; he commanded, and it stood fast" (Psalm 33:9).

When we go to nature, what do we see? Almost infinite variety, but also discernible patterns, structure, purpose. We notice some unquestionable adaptation and modification. We see some degree of cruelty in the animal world, unnecessary multiplication, and some confusion amid general order. The face of nature is not all beautiful, nor bountiful. Is that a problem? It certainly is a problem, but these negative elements need not surprise us. Although we may not be able to explain all the details, the problem of sin and rebellion by one who stood high in divine councils would seem to adequately explain the present state of our earth.

But what does creation tell us about God? We must press to that main point. The people who study space and the planets, moons, and stars scattered through it talk of time and space dimensions that make the mind swim. Well, if God is the architect of all of that, it tells us something about His greatness, His wisdom, His power, and His vast domain. Inspiration speaks of space as "illimitable" (*The Great Controversy,* p. 678). And how big is that?

At the other end of the scale, the theories of atomic physics talk about a universe within the atom. What does that tell us about God? It leaves us a little uncomprehending, but surely we cannot doubt His ability to care for infinite minutiae of detail. Should we doubt that He has numbered the hairs of our head or that He knows when a common sparrow drops injured or lifeless to the ground?

We find in God's universe—despite sin—a remarkable level of reliability and predictability. Every scientist operates on the premise that the universe operates in so orderly a manner that it can be described and will retain its qualities and characteristics. As I write, the robins are back, the cardinals are back, and some of the warblers are on the move. I usually hear the Canada geese and then see their high V's each autumn and spring. God is a God of order, of law.

Nature also tells us some deeply spiritual and loving things about God. For example, there is the tender care many creatures bestow on their young. Some may call this devotion instinct rather than love and see it as merely a drive to preserve the species. One's interpretation depends upon one's presuppositions, doesn't it? Evolutionists would read only the latter in it. Those who believe in a Creator could read it as a level of love.

Was it merely coincidental that the Carpenter of Nazareth drew so many of His lessons on love and righteousness from the plants, animals, and trees of Judea and Galilee? Or are there indeed illustrations of the spiritual in the physical realm, the natural world reflecting in some measure the eternal world? "Ever since the creation of the world his invisible nature, namely, his eternal power and deity, has been clearly perceived in the things that have been made" (Romans 1:20, RSV).

But there is one distinct limitation to the witness of nature to the God of nature. "The deepest students of science are constrained to recognize in nature the working of infinite power. But to man's unaided reason, nature's teaching cannot but be contradictory and disappointing. Only in the light of revelation can it be read aright. 'Through faith we understand.' Hebrews 11:3.

" 'In the beginning God.' Genesis 1:1. Here alone can the mind in its eager questioning, fleeing as the dove to the ark, find rest. Above, beneath, beyond, abides Infinite Love, working out all things to accomplish 'the good pleasure of His goodness.' 2 Thessalonians 1:11.

" 'The invisible things of Him since the creation of the world are . . . perceived through the things that are made, even His everlasting power and divinity.' Romans 1:20, R.V. But their testimony can be understood only through the aid of the divine Teacher. 'What man knoweth the things of a man, save the spirit of man which is in him? even so the things of God knoweth no man but the Spirit of God.' 1 Corinthians 2:11.

" 'When He, the Spirit of truth, is come, He will guide you into all truth.' John 16:13. Only by the aid of that Spirit who in the beginning 'was brooding upon the face of the waters;' of that Word by whom 'all things were made;' of that 'true Light, which lighteth every man that cometh into the world,' can the testimony of science be rightly interpreted. Only by their guidance can its deepest truths be discerned.

"Only under the direction of the Omniscient One shall we, in the study of His works, be enabled to think His thoughts after Him" (*Education,* p. 134).

General revelation—the witness to God of the natural world—constantly needs the insights and clarification which come from special revelation—the witness of the Spirit of truth to the truth regarding God, man, the universe, and all their vital interrelationships. It takes little consideration to recognize in nature antagonistic forms and powers—life and death, health and disease, growth and decay, giving and taking, abundance and dearth, tenderness and cruelty, intelligence and insanity. And the list could go on.

We also need constantly to remember the impact of sin upon ourselves and our capacities—we have greater difficulty now in reading aright God's revelation of Himself through the channel of nature.

"Before the Fall, not a cloud rested upon the minds of our first parents to obscure their clear perception of the character of God. They were perfectly conformed to the will of God. For a covering, a beautiful light, the light of God, surrounded them. The Lord visited the holy pair, and instructed them through the works of His hands. Nature was their lesson book. In the Garden of Eden the existence of God was demonstrated in the objects of nature that surrounded them. Every tree of the garden spoke to them. The invisible things of God were clearly seen, being understood by the things which were made, even His eternal power and Godhead.

"But while it is true that God could thus be discerned in nature, this does not favor the assertion that after the Fall a perfect knowledge of God was revealed in the natural world to Adam and his posterity. Nature could convey her lessons to man in his innocence; but transgression brought a blight upon nature, and intervened between nature and nature's God. Had Adam and Eve never disobeyed their Creator, had they remained in the path of perfect rectitude, they could have known and understood God. But when they listened to the voice of the tempter, and sinned against God, the light of the garments of heavenly innocence departed from them; and in parting with the garments of innocence, they drew about them the dark robes of ignorance of God. The clear and perfect light that had hitherto surrounded them had lightened everything they approached; but deprived of that heavenly light, the posterity of Adam could no longer trace the character of God in His created works" (*Selected Messages,* Book One, pp. 290, 291).

We must constantly learn the humiliating lesson of our own inefficiency in reading nature correctly. As we become increasingly sophisticated in our technology and are able to amass vast quantities of data, the conviction grows stronger that we can unlock the secrets of the universe. And as far as observable data is concerned we very much can, but when it comes to the history of nature and the work of nature's God, He remains to many the "unknown God" of the Athenians. "He is unknown to all who, without the guidance of the divine Teacher, take up the study of nature" (*Testimonies,* Vol. 8, p. 257).

Almost as a footnote to this chapter, we wish to comment on a method that is used by those who think they see conflicts between the Bible's testimony about God and His works and the evidences of nature or science. It is a method used also to explain the teachings of the Bible that do not harmonize with the presuppositions with which men come to its study. To illustrate, if a typically modern person assumes (with the average scientist and historian) that there are no miracles, then he has to do something about the many claimed miracles in the Bible. So what does he do? He probably points out that every writer is "historically conditioned," which means that the writer reflects the prevailing views and understandings of his time and is even limited to the ideas, concepts, and language of his age.

Did his contemporaries believe in miracles? Then it is natural that he will reflect such a belief. Did his contemporaries believe in a fiat creation and a short history of man? He will reflect this view, even if he is an inspired writer. So to resolve the conflict, someone must reinterpret what the inspired person wrote so that it will harmonize with present-day knowledge. Thus it is argued that Genesis was not written to be a realistic account of origins. It is reinterpreted as expressing a relationship between man and God that would set the spiritual framework of the Bible story.

At the outset we must acknowledge that every person to a degree reflects his own times, and without doubt each inspired writer has his own unique vocabulary and style. Unless one assumes that the Bible writers were God's *pen* rather than His *penmen,* there will be the impress of the individual's language capacity in his writing. But as we shall see in Chapter 6, the resultant revelation is still the Word of God.

Then again, the New Testament writers saw depth of meaning in Old Testament statements that would not be obvious by any regular analysis of the language. So there is a type of reinterpretation here. And an Ellen White might reinterpret both the Old and New Testaments. But the vital factor here is that the reinterpreter is also an inspired writer. The Holy Spirit is the virtual Author of all inspired writings.

Without the qualification of inspiration, *anyone* could assume the role of reinterpreter, and in secular writings that might not be a problem. However, when the authority of the Bible is based on its inspiration, then *un*inspired reinterpretation of the Bible could involve a breakdown in the authority of inspired writings. It is difficult to see how such a process of reinterpretation would have any definable limits. Where would the process stop?

Reinterpretation is such a common practice in contemporary theology and in modern efforts to help the Bible conform to modern science that the believer in the Bible as God's authoritative self-revelation needs to be aware of the phenomenon and to consider its implications. He needs to remember also that all human knowledge is fraught with limitations. The facts of science or history today sometimes have to be modified or discarded tomorrow in the light of further evidence. In terms of origins, the Bible offers as valid a model as any—and in many respects (and certainly for the believer in the self-revealing God) a vastly superior model.

We turn now to God's revelation through His great acts in human history.

CHAPTER IV

GOD SPEAKS BY WHAT HE DOES

Theologians speak impressively of God's *salvific* acts in human history. They refer to Him as the "acting God," because He has broken into human history and intervened in the affairs of men and nations. Not all theologians, by any means, hold this view of God —any more than all acknowledge Him to be the Creator and Sustainer of the universe. The Bible, however, is unequivocal in its portrayal of God as the acting, intervening God who seeks to save the human race. Not only does the Bible relate these acts of God, but it explains His purposes behind them, which we might not discover without such divine revelations.

We cannot here omit Creation from God's great acts even though the previous chapter concentrated on it, and this reference provides opportunity to bring out its salvific dimension. When God created this world and the human family, He thereby committed Himself to all that has been and is involved in our salvation. The possibility of rebellion lay inherent in the moral capacity with which God endowed us. The presence of the great deceiver in the universe made our deception a possibility, though God thoroughly warned and instructed our first parents regarding the danger and the means for escaping it. In the last analysis our sovereign will implicated the Godhead in Calvary and all that it represents. So Creation rightly heads the list of God's salvific acts. It happened first, and it carried within it the potential for calling up all the subsequent saving acts of God.

Another way to look at Creation is to consider what its results would have been had the first parents chosen God's will in preference to their own. In one sense we would have had by Creation what can now be ours only by redemption and re-creation. This is not the whole story, of course, because God plans to do even more for us now than

He intended in the original plan. (No, it was not a good thing that we sinned. But where sin abounded, grace did much more abound.) So we could think of Creation as a saving act even if there had been no Fall.

But now we move on swiftly over a span of some two thousand years, for Scripture or any other source of information relates little about them. Presumably, what occurred in the centuries leading up to the Flood is not essential to our understanding of the acting, saving God. And so we come to the Flood—one facet of God's "strange work" (Isaiah 28:21)—as He takes from an entire generation, less eight souls, His own gift of life. Can we imagine how Heaven wept with the falling rain and broke up in sympathy with the fountains of the great deep as they began their destructive work?

But what does the Flood tell us about God? How does it form a part of His self-revelation? There are the rather obvious dimensions—His power, His ability to meet any crisis, His direct control of bird and beast (as they entered and remained in the ark). But then there are less-obvious dimensions—two thousand years of working, pleading, and waiting for our ancestors to choose His will and way rather than destruction; His meticulous attention to detail in the design and composition of the ark; His complete openness and fairness in warning the final generation of their impending doom by every hammer blow upon the rising structure of the ark; His grace in taking Noah and his sons and their wives into the ark—for although they believed and acted out their faith in God's word, they were far from mature saints in whom the processes of sanctification were complete; His utter devotion to His goal of preserving a line of descendants upon the earth through whom the Promised Seed of the woman would come—the pre-flood condition of the race would suggest to us a profligate people worthy of abandonment; God's willingness to adapt His plans to our changing needs and situations—the fear of man placed upon the wild beasts and the permission to add flesh to the diet; the assurance of seedtime and harvest; the abbreviation of the life-span. These, and many other aspects of the Flood, if we knew and understood them, tell us of God's love and power. But we have more ground to cover.

It would be tempting to spend time on God's other great acts between the Flood and the Exodus. We could probe the revelation of

God in the Tower of Babel experience, the call and journeys of Abram, the birth and accepted sacrifice of Isaac, the work of God's grace on the heart and life of Jacob, the tragedies and providences in the life of Joseph, or the descent of Jacob and his sons into Egypt and God's care for them in all their situations. But we wish to take a longer look at the Exodus which, after all, grew out of much that we have just listed.

We cannot comprehend the Exodus for all that it is without recognizing the place of covenants in God's dealings with the seed of Abraham. But even if we understand that correctly, many aspects of the Exodus are not yet well explained. And, of course, those who deny the possibility of miracles look for natural causes of what Moses describes, or they reinterpret what Moses wrote to explain away the seeming miracles.

We cannot easily explain just how the Lord divided the sea to bring Israel through and then drowned the Egyptian host. How He handled the sheer logistics (if we have anything like a correct view of the size of the marching multitudes) of the situation within the time period given defies human accounting. (Think how fast refugees can travel today with their bundles and trundles.) But there it is (the Exodus), and there they are (the Jews), and history cannot easily ignore them.

Some wonder why secular history has not more to say about God's great acts in the Exodus, but the ancient kings rarely recorded their defeats in war with each other, let alone at the hands of a denied God and His hated followers. Be that as it may, there may be more than poetry to God's assertion at the covenant-making: "You have seen what I did to the Egyptians, and how I bore you on eagles' wings and brought you to myself" (Exodus 19:4, RSV).

The Christian historian can always remember that in the kingdom "there will be open to the student, history of infinite scope and of wealth inexpressible. Here, from the vantage ground of God's word, the student is afforded a view of the vast field of history and may gain some knowledge of the principles that govern the course of human events. But his vision is still clouded, and his knowledge incomplete. Not until he stands in the light of eternity will he see all things clearly.

"Then will be opened before him the course of the great conflict that had its birth before time began, and that ends only when time shall cease. The history of the inception of sin; of fatal falsehood in its crooked working; of truth that, swerving not from its own straight lines, has met and conquered error—all will be made manifest. The veil that interposes between the visible and the invisible world will be drawn aside, and wonderful things will be revealed'' (*Education,* p. 304).

The fact remains that the Exodus was epochal in the experience of Israel. It formed the point of reference for major and minor prophets alike and was the subject of magnificent Hebrew psalms (see Psalms 78, 105, 106, 135, 136, 147). Israel's whole history received its impetus from the Exodus, and it was a matter of God's continual concern that they should not forget it and what it revealed about Him.

From the Exodus onward, Israel became a nation directly involved with the great and small countries on every side. Had she only remembered the Exodus and trusted God, the stories written by Isaiah, Jeremiah, Ezekiel, Daniel, and the minor prophets would have been different.

That brief paragraph covers the tragic years of the divided monarchy, the captivities, the pathetically small return, and the four hundred years during which Inspiration closes the book, as it were, and awaits the coming of the One like Moses.

Types, symbols, and particularly the sacrificial system of the Old Testament prefigure Jesus Christ, and His first advent brought the reality they had promised. He sealed the promises of the covenants, and His coming gave to us and to the universe the crowning revelation of God's character. Undeniably in Him, God is love.

But He is not here. He has returned to God's throne. So who will represent Him now, who will speak for Him? Since He came as man to reveal God to us, is there no longer such a man-witness? Yes, there is indeed. Endowed and instructed by the Holy Spirit, those whom Christ had chosen as His closest followers became His human successors. Note these significant words: ''How shall we escape, if we neglect so great salvation; which at the first began to be spoken by the Lord, and was confirmed unto us by them that heard him?'' (Hebrews 2:3).

The eyewitnesses of Jesus became the nucleus of His church, the body of called-out ones who believed the apostles' testimony concerning Jesus of Nazareth. And really, these people, the church, became, from Pentecost to the end of this age, the main channel of God's self-revelation. So declares the Word of God: "That through the church the manifold wisdom of God might now be made known to the principalities and powers in the heavenly places" (Ephesians 3:10, RSV).

And the church leads us to God's final great act in the restoration of the kingdom planned from the foundation of the world—the kingdom of glory. In Eden, our first parents had enjoyed open communion with the Creator, and God will restore that joy. He made them in His image, and by the time of the final triumph He will have restored that image. The process is at work even now in His church.

Does all this say something about what God is like? Can we see that God reveals Himself by what He does, from the beginning to the end of this present age? And all for those who, wise in their own wisdom, listened to the voice of the serpent! Who can measure or explain such love? Really, we cannot stop at the restoration and feel that we shall then have learned all there is to know of the self-revealing God—not by any means. From that day forward we shall drink the water of life and partake of the fruits of the tree of life freely. And there will never be an end, for although God's salvific acts terminate in the establishment of the kingdom of glory, we shall spend all eternity plumbing the depths of the love that gave birth to His actions. "I will rejoice in Jerusalem, and joy in my people" (Isaiah 65:19).

While we live, work, and pray for the day when "we shall ever feel the freshness of the morning, and shall ever be far from its close" (*The Great Controversy,* p. 676), let us now contemplate the glory of God revealed in the face of Jesus Christ our Lord.

CHAPTER V

GOD SPEAKS SUPREMELY IN CHRIST

We might be tempted to ask, perhaps with some petulant self-pity, "How could it be otherwise, that God would speak supremely in Christ? After all, wasn't He God?" In His conflict with sin, no. Neither was He exactly man as we are. But through all the mystery of His coming to dwell among us and being one with us, one thing remains clear and certain: He was "one who in every respect has been tempted as we are, yet without sinning" (Hebrews 4:15, RSV). Jesus endured temptations of a kind and at a level that we can never know. But clinging to the arm of His Father by faith and empowered by the indwelling of the same Holy Spirit who will indwell us, He lived in humanity a life that perfectly revealed God.

But let us go back and ask ourselves why Christ had to be so poor, so humble, if He came here to reveal the great God of the universe whose work we have extolled in Chapter 3. The answer embraces a number of parts, and we shall doubtless not cover them all here. In the first place, the Gospels assert that "the common people heard him gladly" (Mark 12:37) and that "the poor . . . [had] the gospel preached to them" (Matthew 11:5). What would have happened if Christ had appeared in affluence? Have you ever been poor and been near the wealthy? Were you attracted? Did you feel they understood you? Jesus took the position of the poorest and humblest to show that human advantage is not the key to being like God.

But there is an opposite factor here. Jesus would not attract by outward appearance. God's glory resides supremely in His character, full of might and majesty though He is. On occasion Jesus permitted His divinity to flash forth, and He was transfigured before three chosen disciples. But He veiled His power and glory so that He might come to live with us without consuming us. Yet He could not veil the beauty of God's love. He came to portray that. The rich and the learned, those of noble birth, must be attracted to God's character and not to the trappings with which they would feel at home.

And still the greatest reason for His humble setting has not been brought forward. Think back to the beginning of Lucifer's problem, which resulted in his full rebellion and open sin. What was the underlying motive for his carefully couched insinuations against God's government and character? According to the symbolism under which Isaiah and Ezekiel portrayed it, he consciously chose to exalt himself. "I will exalt myself." "I will be like the Most High." And the prophet then laments, "How art thou cast down!"

Do you notice how it was with Jesus when He came? Born in a stable. Dependent on the gifts of the Magi for traveling to Egypt. A member of a carpenter's family, with early loss of the bread-winning carpenter. Dependent throughout His ministry upon the hospitality of others. Rode to triumph on a borrowed donkey. Celebrated the Passover in a borrowed room. Was buried in someone else's tomb in donated burial garments. And when He died, the soldiers cast lots for His one piece of personal property—His outer garment. Why?

Just as "up-steppingness" filled Lucifer's heart, so, to an infinitely greater degree, "down-steppingness"* filled Christ's heart. Why? Because God is like that. Jesus came to reveal the most vital aspects of God's glorious character. "But I am among you as one who serves" (Luke 22:27, RSV). There it is. That is God.

God's down-steppingness led Him to make creatures with an intellect, a will, and a consequent moral capacity. It involved an awful personal risk for God, but He did it anyway. And can we assume other than that the Godhead foresaw the inevitable risk? Could that be one reason why Scripture calls Christ "the Lamb slain from the foundation of the world" (Revelation 13:8; see 1 Peter 1:19, 20)?

Christ manifested "alterocentricity" in contrast to Lucifer's "egocentricity." And it was not an attitude Jesus put on merely to negate Lucifer's way, for Jesus could not have acted any other way—that's the way God *is*. Nowhere do we see this more clearly

---

*For the concepts of the down-steppingness of God, the writer is indebted to his friend, Dr. Carsten Johnsen, author of *Man, the Indivisible* (Oslo: Universitetforlaget, 1971).

outlined than in Paul's epistle to the church at Philippi. In Philippians 2:5-11 we can see and hear and feel the steps down that Jesus took, one by one, to be our Saviour and to reveal God to us:

1. He did not count equality with God a thing to be grasped.
2. He emptied Himself.
3. He took the form of a servant.
4. He was born in the likeness of men.
5. Being found in human form, He humbled Himself.
6. He became obedient unto death.
7. He died the death of the cross.

Perhaps you are wondering why the frequent stress in these chapters on the revelation of what God is like. It is a vital matter because it affects the only rationale for the distinction between the treatment of Lucifer and his fellow rebels and the treatment of mankind. Why should God give us a "second chance" but not the fallen angels? Lucifer and those who joined him in rebellion against God's government transgressed with a full revelation of God's character before them. Adam and Eve transgressed under a situation complicated by satanic deception and without the same degree of God's self-revelation the fallen angels knew. God could reveal no more of His character to Lucifer in the hope of regaining his allegiance, although He gave him the opportunity to reconsider and return. But if God could reveal to man His character in its depth of love and down-steppingness, perhaps He could regain man's loyalty and restore him to fellowship.

"But even as a sinner, man was in a different position from that of Satan. Lucifer in heaven had sinned in the light of God's glory. To him as to no other created being was given a revelation of God's love. Understanding the character of God, knowing His goodness, Satan chose to follow his own selfish, independent will. This choice was final. There was no more that God could do to save him. But man was deceived; his mind was darkened by Satan's sophistry. The height and depth of the love of God he did not know. For him there was hope in a knowledge of God's love. By beholding His character he might be drawn back to God" (*The Desire of Ages,* pp. 761, 762).

Heartrending and also revelatory of God's wonderful love is the inspired account of an interview which Satan sought with Christ: "Satan trembled as he viewed his work. He was alone in meditation upon the past, the present, and his future plans. His mighty frame shook as with a tempest. An angel from heaven was passing. He called him and entreated an interview with Christ. This was granted him. He then related to the Son of God that he repented of his rebellion and wished again the favor of God. He was willing to take the place God had previously assigned him, and be under His wise command. Christ wept at Satan's woe but told him, as the mind of God, that he could never be received into heaven. Heaven must not be placed in jeopardy. All heaven would be marred should he be received back, for sin and rebellion originated with him. The seeds of rebellion were still within him. He had, in his rebellion, no occasion for his course, and he had hopelessly ruined not only himself but the host of angels also, who would then have been happy in heaven had he remained steadfast. The law of God could condemn but could not pardon'' (*The Story of Redemption,* p. 26).

Into our world, dominated by Satan's influence over the majority, the Son of God came to reflect God's glory and to bear ''the very stamp of his nature'' (Hebrews 1:3, RSV). Christ came to portray in the flesh God's character. So completely did He succeed in this venture that He could tell His disciples, ''If you have seen Me, you have seen the Father'' (see John 14:9).

Understandably, therefore, the Christ who came to redeem man will also judge those whom He came to save but who chose to believe not. He who wept over Lucifer's banishment from heaven and who suffered the second death to deliver us from Satan's grasp will be as faithful a judge as He has been a merciful and faithful High Priest in the heavenly sanctuary. Soon He will lay aside His priestly garments and clothe Himself for the work of judgment.

The fact that judgment has been so long delayed testifies to God's patience, His desire to save everyone possible, and His awareness of the awful doom to fall upon the finally impenitent. But even in the final judgment, Christ will reveal God, for God cannot condone rebellion against His law, His character, and His government. To tolerate rebellion would mean to deny His holy and righteous character, of which the moral law is a transcription fitted to the needs and circumstances of the human family.

''And God 'hath given Him authority to execute judgment also, because He is the Son of man.' Because He has tasted the very dregs of human affliction and temptation, and understands the frailties and sins of men; because in our behalf He has victoriously withstood the temptations of Satan, and will deal justly and tenderly with the souls that His own blood has been poured out to save—because of this, the Son of man is appointed to execute the judgment'' (*The Desire of Ages*, p. 210).

So Jesus pleads with sinners and gives the Holy Spirit and ministering angels to impress our hearts with an awareness of guilt, to give us a spirit of repentance, and to assure us of God's forgiving grace. The same Jesus wept over an impenitent city and people: ''How can I give thee up?'' Although we have repulsed, ignored, and denied Him, His heart of love is breaking. He longs to forgive, longs to reclaim. He uses every figure, parable, and illustration to convey His compassion and yearning for our salvation. ''Behold, I stand at the door, and knock'' (Revelation 3:20).

When I ''colporteured'' in Britain, where every man's home, however humble, was his castle, I often saw the curtains moving after I had knocked at the door. I knew that someone was there. In fact, sometimes I could look right into the living room or down the hallway, if the door stood ajar, and see the owner sitting or standing there. I would sometimes knock again on the door knocker, a little more distinctly perhaps, or push the doorbell again—or both. Yet they acted as though I were not there. But can we do this to the Creator of the vast universe, the King of kings and Lord of all lords? How can we act as though He were not there? ''Freely will He pardon all who come to Him for forgiveness and restoration'' (*ibid.*, p. 568). Shall we answer His knock, today?

We have no idea how much Jesus suffered in His daily contact with sinners. He could have called hosts of angels to comfort and aid Him had He chosen, but, no, His was one of the loneliest lives ever lived on this earth, as far as human understanding and fellowship were concerned. His closest friends could sleep during His crises, and those of His family were among His worst critics.

In Gethsemane we most clearly see God revealed in Christ. All the planning for that hour and the pre-Creation agreements with the Father were almost as nothing now. No past experience of time or of eternity was adequate for this. As a human being He viewed eternity past by faith and revelation only. He had laid aside His divine prerogatives. "Christ was now standing in a different attitude from that in which He had ever stood before. His suffering can best be described in the words of the prophet, 'Awake, O sword, against My shepherd, and against the man that is My fellow, saith the Lord of hosts.' Zechariah 13:7. As the substitute and surety for sinful man, Christ was suffering under divine justice. He saw what justice meant. Hitherto He had been as an intercessor for others; now He longed to have an intercessor for Himself" (*ibid.*, p. 686).

Here the decision of the ages was actually sealed. Calvary but implemented the agony of Gethsemane. Jesus was preserved in the Garden to die on the cross. And that is what God is like. He has spoken.

CHAPTER VI

GOD SPEAKS TO MEN THROUGH MEN

We have already pointed to God's great condescension in making men His channels of communication and self-revelation. While we do not know the language of heaven, we can speak in the medium that we do know. This does not suggest that God needs a person to translate into our languages for Him, but in His great love He gives men and women the privilege of speaking for Him. And the miracle of it all is that He portrays the product as the Word of God.

When we begin to chip away at the truthfulness of that last statement, we move on to new and difficult ground. If we ever attempt to classify or categorize the various parts of the inspired whole, distinguishing this portion as "more inspired" and that portion as "less inspired," we would be setting up our own external norms by which to judge the Bible, thus denying its self-authentication. In the past, that road has led in only one direction and to only one destination—the abandonment of the inspiration of Scripture that gives it authority and makes and keeps it self-authenticating.

Ellen G. White was remarkably consistent and unequivocal in instructing us—the church—*not* to get into the business of classifying one portion of the Bible as inspired and another not. She could scarcely have spoken more directly or specifically: Cling to your Bible, brethren, and take it just as it reads. Obey it, and not one of you will be lost! (see *Selected Messages,* Book One, p. 18). The more we look at what has happened over the past century or two to those who have moved from this committed position, the more we are convinced of her sound advice.

This chapter deals with God's process of communicating with His chosen human channels. We are here arbitrarily distinguishing between revelation and the process of inspiration by which God guides

His servants in transmitting to others what He has communicated.

We have intimated earlier in the book that it involves some mysteries. As a student of communications, I find some things difficult to understand, let alone explain. But I have similar problems in other areas of knowledge—whether secular or spiritual. (And I find that the best-informed in all areas do also and readily admit it.)

For example, I cannot adequately explain how God conveyed *thoughts* to His prophets while allowing them to choose the words. I do not understand how a thought can be transmitted other than through some kind of code such as language—a code which must be adequately matched between the sender and the receiver. For communicators, a thought is something of an internalized and abbreviated conversation with oneself. Do we think without words or their equivalent?

Some will say, "The Lord showed His prophets something, and they used their *own* words to describe it." Yes, I can see *that* in the prophetic and apocalyptic portions of the Bible, but there are other considerable portions. Some will begin to wonder whether the writer has lost faith or compromised confidence in the Word. No, that is not the situation. Acknowledging problems does not necessarily mean denying faith. Of course, if we go around collecting and magnifying the problems, we begin to lean toward a heart of unbelief.

Some Christians have resolved some of these and similar problems by resorting to the kind of "verbal inspiration" that makes the prophet God's pen, not His penman. But that solution only creates other and greater problems. The most extreme position is perhaps illustrated by those sincere souls (and they may well be among the finally redeemed) who insist that only the King James Version of the Bible was and is inspired. Such dedication to literalness overlooks the fact that the Scriptures were written in Hebrew, Aramaic, and Greek, rather than in English. (But God has overlooked much greater human misunderstandings than this.)

Seventh-day Adventists have a unique advantage over many other Christians, for we believe that God spoke to and through Ellen G. White by the same means He used to speak to the Bible writers. So we have the great advantage of her comparatively recent experience, her considerable description of that experience, and her insights into the revelation-inspiration phenomenon.

Before reviewing some of these insights, let us point out that God is not limited by our understanding of the communication process. Because *we* do not know how thought can be conveyed without the source determining the code or language in which the thought is couched does not mean that God has not some other way. The language used in transmitting the message to us is generally that of the prophet (the receiver) except when he quotes God's words.

Even though we expect that the reader may have read them before, the following paragraphs are so pertinent to this chapter that we wish to quote them here: "The Bible is written by inspired men, but it is not God's mode of thought and expression. It is that of humanity. God, as a writer, is not represented. Men will often say such an expression is not like God. But God has not put Himself in words, in logic, in rhetoric, on trial in the Bible. The writers of the Bible were God's penmen, not His pen. Look at the different writers.

"It is not the words of the Bible that are inspired, but the men that were inspired. Inspiration acts not on the man's words or his expressions but on the man himself, who, under the influence of the Holy Ghost, is imbued with *thoughts*. But the *words* receive the impress of the individual mind. The divine mind is diffused. The divine mind and will is combined with the human mind and will; thus the utterances of the man *are the word of God*" (*ibid.*, p. 21, italics supplied).

Perhaps the statement that "the divine mind and will is combined with the human mind and will" comes as close as possible to explaining the process of God's self-revelation.

"Through the inspiration of His Spirit the Lord gave His apostles truth, to be expressed according to the development of their minds by the Holy Spirit. But the mind is not cramped, as if forced into a certain mold.

"The Lord speaks to human beings in imperfect speech, in order that the degenerate senses, the dull, earthly perception, of earthly beings may comprehend His words. Thus is shown God's condescension. He meets fallen human beings where they are. The Bible, perfect as it is in its simplicity, does not answer to the great ideas of God; for infinite ideas cannot be perfectly embodied in finite vehicles of thought. Instead of the expressions of the Bible being exaggerated, as many people suppose, the strong expessions break down before the magnificence of the thought, though the penman selected the most expressive language through which to convey the truths of higher education. Sinful beings can only bear to look upon a shadow of the brightness of heaven's glory'' (*ibid.*, p. 22).

We have spent a considerable portion of this chapter discussing the role of human beings in God's self-revelation because this has proved the most crucial area of Biblical criticism—crucial in the sense that it has led to the steady erosion of the Bible's authority as God's Word. However, the reader should study this and the following chapter together, because they are two faces of a single process. In some respects there is no great point in distinguishing the two parts, but it gives us opportunity to see the different aspects more distinctly. We will observe here only that the difficulties we may have in understanding *how* God communicated His self-revelation are met in and safeguarded by the assurance that the same Holy Spirit who gave the revelation supervised the writing of the Scriptures—a process which we are arbitrarily calling inspiration.

But let's resume our present theme. Just to illustrate the Bible's own awareness (if we may speak thus of a book) of its being the Word of God, observe how frequently it intimates such. For example, we find 361 times the phrase ''the utterance of the Lord'' in the Old Testament. ''Thus says the Lord'' or variations of it appear some 445 times. Variations on ''word of God,'' indicating divine communication in commandments, prophecy, and words of instruction, appear in some 540 instances. Those who received these words (orally at first, many times) apparently understood that the messenger was speaking for God and not merely as a human being. Jesus Himself never doubted the authority of the Old Testament—the only portion of the Bible with which He worked (see Matthew 5:17-19; Luke 10:25-28; 16:19-31).

Now, because the Bible often repeats its claim to be the Word of God does not mean that the numerical fact alone proves anything. It does indicate clearly, however, the light in which the Biblical writers wished to be seen.

As far as the New Testament is concerned, it comes with the predictions and revelations of the Old Testament behind it, plus the supreme authority of Jesus Christ Himself, the divine *Logos* (see Hebrews 1:1 and John 1:1-5). We find the combined and parallel authority of the living and written New Testament persistently illustrated. A careful word study with the aid of a standard concordance supports this claim. For example: Salvation is in Jesus (Acts 4:12; 2 Timothy 2:10; Hebrews 2:10; 5:9) and the Word (Acts 13:26; compare Ephesians 1:13). So with life, grace, reconciliation, and truth. The Inspired Word carried with it Jesus' authority.

We have mentioned here and there that Biblical criticism has deprived many Christians of the confidence they once had in the authority of the Scripture. For many young people, it has prevented them from ever considering the claims of the Bible to be God's self-revelation. In an over-simplified way we can say that Biblical criticism is involved here because, in spite of its often-good intentions, it has accepted the assumptions and presuppositions of the critic of secular history, philosophy, science, and literature. Biblical critics have insisted that the same standards and tests used in these altogether human disciplines should apply also to the study and evaluation of the Bible. This we may speak of as the negative side of Biblical criticism.

On the positive side, we can cheerfully acknowledge that Biblical criticism has helped us arrive at a more accurate text of the Bible in the original languages. It has given us keys to many Biblical words, expressions, idioms, and even customs through the study of the cultures and languages close to the peoples who are the subject of Scripture. It has rid us of the many fantastic and unnecessary claims by those who accepted without question the interpretations and dogmas of the Middle Ages when a "universal" church arbitrarily decided what was truth. For these gifts of Biblical criticism we are grateful.

When, however, any man presupposes that there is no such thing as a miracle, that God cannot intervene in human history, that evolution is the only valid theory of origins, that Christianity is only one among many spiritual achievements of the human family, that religious thought evolves as all other human progress evolves, and that Israel's religion copied that of the surrounding nations—then we have problems and a parting of the ways.

Possibly an optimistic person reading thus far will suggest, "Perhaps the Adventist Church can prove the exception that puts the rule to the test." Perhaps, because of our strong tradition for the authority of the Bible and the work of Ellen G. White among us, we could accept and work with the presuppositions of Biblical criticism and derive only the benefits.

"Well," says another, "let us not accept the presuppositions of the Biblical critic, but let us use his methodology." That sounds good, too, for we want an accurate text of the Bible—as accurate as possible. We want sound backgrounds on Bible times and events, the help of history, geography, archaeology, and other such fields. Yes, so far that sounds very good. But can we use the Biblical critic's methodology without becoming imperceptibly influenced by his presuppositions? Presuppositions are the "givens," the postulates, the assumptions with which people in all fields of learning start out. The present methodology of any field of knowledge is the outgrowth, the product, the consequence of its presuppositions.

Obviously, we must exercise supreme caution here. Let us mention one other aspect that could make the Biblical critic's work appear worthy of consideration by Seventh-day Adventists and all other earnest Christians. A number of the keymen in modern liberal studies of the Bible had a noble objective (and we do not question their sincerity in seeking it) when they began their critical studies. They stated, "We live in a scientific, educated age. Critical capacities are being developed which lead people to think that they cannot accept or retain faith in the gospel of Jesus Christ. We must find a way to make this gospel *relevant* to this modern, scientific age. We must find language for it that will make sense to this generation."

Now who could ask for a more timely objective? But there were problems. In their effort to make the Bible and the gospel relevant to a rationalistic, scientific age, keymen in liberal theology not only adjusted the *language* of the gospel but also changed the *gospel* itself. Although sometimes they retained a few of the old gospel terms, they had given them new meanings.

We may have mentioned earlier that out of the age of rationalism and the enlightenment, critical studies of literature, history, music, and other fields developed. The leading lights of the day then began to say, "The Bible is also a piece of old literature and history, and we should approach it and test it by the same standards." This approach led to several types of criticism: (1) literary criticism, (2) form criticism, and (3) tradition criticism. The first attempted to discover the documents or sources assumed to lie behind the text. The second sought the structure and the life setting that produced a given structure in the text. The last considered the history of the processes that modified and synthesized the supposed original sources of the Bible and especially wished to discover the motivation for the various stages of change that led to the final form in Scripture.

In this climate and context modern liberal theologians and Biblical critics conduct their studies. They take these concepts and approaches for granted. But with this great emphasis upon the human aspects of the development of Scripture, the divine element becomes secondary, at least, if not completely overlooked. It virtually nullifies the revelational dimension of the Holy Scriptures.

Now we need to look at the process of inspiration.

CHAPTER VII

GOD'S MEN RECORD WHAT HE SAYS AND DOES

Existential theologians often wish to limit God's role in the Scriptures and in the development of Christianity to an encounter between God and the prophet of which the prophet later speaks. This encounter, however, does not transmit data, because it supposedly lies beyond the "information barrier." There is a self-disclosure of God to man, but not the transmission of truths about *God*. Scholars who hold this view concede that Scripture may *witness* to God's self-revelation, but they do not consider the Bible to be concerned with doctrine or a self-revelation of God.

Now this simply is not the traditional, historical Protestant approach to the Word of God, and Seventh-day Adventists should measure these various approaches and determine where we shall stand in relation to them.

If the Bible records only the prophet's later reflections on his experience of God's presence or if it results from a unique stimulation of his spiritual faculties, then Christianity ceases to be a *revealed* religion. We say "ceases to be" in the sense that until modern times, no Christian denied that God had revealed truths about Himself, man, and the universe.

Only a short step from the encounter concept of the Bible leads to the view which not only sees Scripture as merely a witness to revelation rather than a revelation but also sees the individual who receives the witness as the one who determines what that witness is, what it says to him, and what in his own experience it stimulates.

From the introduction of this book onward, we have insisted that we cannot "find" God, nor can we probe the reasons for our existence. We have offered, instead, the God who is not silent. Indeed, God's transcendence demands such a revelation if we are to know

Him. We have asserted that although God has spoken through the things which He has made and through His salvific acts in history, we need His interpretation of these events and acts if we are to read them correctly. We have portrayed both the Living Word and the Written Word as His prime channels of self-revelation.

We have seen the advantages in God's speaking to us through theophanies (manifestations of God to man), visions, dreams, and even the remarkably open relationships given by God to Moses (see Numbers 12:1-4; Deuteronomy 34:10). Now we come to "inspiration," that aspect by which the prophet or other chosen messenger both receives and transmits the divine self-revelation. It falls within our limited understanding that the God who reveals Himself to us also superintends the transmission of the message to us by His messenger.

We cannot assume, however, that because of this divine supervision of God's revelation we now have all truth—that there is nothing beyond what has been revealed. We see partially as one would see reflections in an inadequate mirror (1 Corinthians 13:12), for only in eternity will we dwell in the light of God's presence. But God has revealed what is essential (John 5:39, 40).

Customarily, then, inspiration refers to the divine origin of the Bible. "All scripture is inspired by God" (2 Timothy 3:16, RSV). "No prophecy ever came by the impulse of man, but men moved by the Holy Spirit spoke from God" (2 Peter 1:21, RSV). The literal meaning of the Greek word *theopneustos* in 2 Timothy 3:16 indicates God's direct action. "Men moved by the Holy Spirit spoke from God." What does that mean? They did not speak "by the impulse of man." The Spirit carried them along so that the resultant words, though theirs, carried His authority.

We are perhaps disappointed that the Bible writers did not fully explain the "how" of inspiration. Possibly even those whom the Spirit "moved" could scarcely describe the experience. "I must boast; there is nothing to be gained by it, but I will go on to visions and revelations of the Lord. I know a man in Christ who fourteen years ago was caught up to the third heaven—whether in the body or out of the body I do not know, God knows. And I know that this man was caught up into Paradise—whether in the body or out of the body I do not know, God knows—and he heard things that cannot be told, which man may not utter" (2 Corinthians 12:1-4, RSV).

If we still feel a little unhappy over the unexplained, let us remind ourselves of the parallel here to the Living Word. How was divinity blended with humanity in Christ? What did the Holy Spirit actually do? Does it matter? Do we really have to know?

To aid us in our limited understanding of inspiration, let us look at another facet of the subject. Some liberal theologians hold quite an exalted concept of the preacher as prophet. With the great emphasis upon individual experience that comes with the existentialist approach to revelation-inspiration, there is the frequent claim that the preacher in his pulpit may be just as much "inspired" as any Biblical writer.

Ellen White answered a similar question about earnest searchers of the Word who lived and worked before we did. Were they inspired? "I dare not say they were not led of God, for Christ leads into all truth; but when it comes to inspiration in the fullest sense of the word, I answer, No. I believe that God has given them a work to do, but if they are not fully consecrated to God at all times, they will weave self and their peculiar traits of character into what they are doing, and will put their mold upon the work, and fashion men in religious experience after their own pattern" (Ellen G. White, *Review and Herald,* March 25, 1890, p. 177).

To hold that every earnest speaker, writer, and Bible student is inspired in the Biblical sense quickly weakens the unique, authoritative mold of the Scriptures as God's self-revelation.

No, the preacher, poet, artist, and musician do not belong in the same class with the Biblical writers who received dreams, visions, symbols, and figures, and "embodied the thought in human language" (*Selected Messages,* Book One, p. 25). The apostle Paul goes so far as to assert that "no one comprehends the thoughts of God except the Spirit of God. Now we have received not the spirit of the world, but the Spirit which is from God, that we might understand the gifts bestowed on us by God. And we impart this in words not taught by human wisdom but taught by the Spirit, interpreting spiritual truths to those who possess the Spirit" (1 Corinthians 2:11-13, RSV).

Here we come to the heart of the chapter and its subject. The Holy Spirit guided the inspired spokesperson in the selection of words by which to impart God's thoughts to Spirit-directed listeners. Ellen G. White confirms this profound and thrilling view: " 'God has been pleased to communicate His truth to the world by human agencies, and He Himself, by His Holy Spirit, qualified men and enabled them to do His work. He guided the mind in the selection of what to speak and what to write. The treasure was entrusted to earthen vessels, yet it is, none the less, from Heaven. The testimony is conveyed through the imperfect expression of human language, yet it is the testimony of God; and the obedient, believing child of God beholds in it the glory of a divine power, full of grace and truth' " (*ibid.,* p. 26).

"At times I am carried far ahead into the future and shown what is to take place. Then again I am shown things as they have occurred in the past. After I come out of vision I do not at once remember all that I have seen, and the matter is not so clear before me until I write, then the scene rises before me as was presented in vision, and I can write with freedom. Sometimes the things which I have seen are hid from me after I come out of vision, and I cannot call them to mind until I am brought before a company where that vision applies, then the things which I have seen come to my mind with force. I am just as dependent upon the Spirit of the Lord in relating or writing a vision, as in having the vision. It is impossible for me to call up things which have been shown me unless the Lord brings them before me at the time that He is pleased to have me relate or write them" (*ibid.,* pp. 36, 37).

In spite of Ellen G. White's strong assertion of dependence on the Holy Spirit in the process of conveying God's message, note the equally strong assertion of the human dimension: "Although I am as dependent upon the Spirit of the Lord in writing my views as I am in receiving them, yet the words I employ in describing what I have seen are my own, unless they be those spoken to me by an angel, which I always enclose in marks of quotation" (*ibid.,* p. 37). This latter statement, if the experience described parallels that of Biblical writers, is as specific as any in countering the accusation of a mechanical, dictational concept of inspiration which is quickly leveled against anyone who sees the Bible as a fully inspired book.

As in our earlier comments on general revelation and special revelation, we are not denying the frailty of the human end of the revelation-inspiration process. No human is infallible. We do not find the prophets claiming infallibility for themselves. Ellen G. White wrote in 1895, "In regard to infallibility, I never claimed it; God alone is infallible." But she went right on to say, "His word is true, and in Him in no variableness, or shadow of turning" (*ibid.).*

On the other hand, Ellen G. White did not deny the possibility of copyists' errors or translators' inaccuracies in the transmission of the Scriptures. She even admits, "This is all probable." But she does not stop there. She goes on to fault "the mind that is so narrow that it will hesitate and stumble over this possibility or probability" because it "would be just as ready to stumble over the mysteries of the Inspired Word, because their feeble minds cannot see through the purposes of God. . . . All the mistakes will not cause trouble to one soul, or cause any feet to stumble, that would not manufacture difficulties from the plainest revealed truth" (*ibid.*, p. 16).

Now when a person has spent a lifetime in textual study of the Scriptures in the original languages, it is quite natural for him to concentrate on the variants—the differences in the available manuscripts, whether of the Old or New Testament. And an uninformed listener might soon assume that there is nothing reliable about the Scriptures as we have them and that the text is as pliable and manipulable as soft wax.

To correct such an impression I wish to quote an old but recognized classic in the field of textual studies. At the close of his chapter on "Variations in the Bible Text," Frederick G. Kenyon, of the Department of Manuscripts of the British Museum, wrote, "No fundamental doctrine of the Christian faith rests on a disputed reading. Constant references to mistakes and divergencies of reading, such as the plan of this book necessitates, might give rise to the doubt whether the substance, as well as the language, of the Bible is not open to question. It cannot be too strongly asserted that in substance the text of the Bible is certain. Especially is this the case with the New Testament.*

"The number of manuscripts of the New Testament, of early translations from it, and of quotations from it in the oldest writers of the Church is so large, that it is practically certain that the true reading of every doubtful passage is preserved in some one or other of these

---

* "Dr. Hort, whose authority on the point is quite incontestable, estimates the proportion of words about which there is *some* doubt at about one-eighth of the whole; but by far the greater part of these consists merely of differences in order and other unimportant variations, and 'the amount of what can in any sense be called substantial variation . . . can hardly form more than a thousandth part of the entire text.' (Introduction to *The New Testament in the Original Greek,* p. 2.)"

ancient authorities. This can be said of no other ancient book in the world. Scholars are satisfied that they possess substantially the true text of the principal Greek and Roman writers whose works have come down to us, of Sophocles, of Thucydides, of Cicero, of Virgil, yet our knowledge of their writings depends on a mere handful of manuscripts, whereas the manuscripts of the New Testament are counted by hundreds, and even thousands.

"In the case of the Old Testament we are not quite in such a good position, as will be shown presently. In some passages it seems certain that the true reading has not been preserved by any ancient authority, and we are driven to conjecture in order to supply it. But such passages are an infinitesimal portion of the whole and may be disregarded. The Christian can take the whole Bible in his hand and say without fear or hesitation that he holds in it the true Word of God, faithfully handed down from generation to generation throughout the centuries" (*Our Bible and the Ancient Manuscripts, A History of the Text and Its Translations,* pp. 10, 11).

As an update on Kenyon's ringing declaration of confidence, we can now point to the 1947 discovery of the Dead Sea Scrolls, which has put in our hands for the first time manuscripts of the Old Testament going back to the time of Jesus and before. The scrolls and fragments date from 250 BC to AD 68, so that we now have Biblical manuscripts about one thousand years older than the oldest Hebrew manuscripts available previously. And the great similarity rather than the differences between the two eras of manuscripts has amazed the scholars. There is a whole new wave of respect for the text of the Old Testament.

As to the New Testament, there are now some 5,500 Greek manuscripts of it in whole or in part, some of which may be considerably less than one hundred years removed from the autograph of John's Gospel. No one need apologize about the reliability of the Biblical text itself. Other literary and historical works whose texts are scarcely questioned or even discussed have not a fraction of the witnesses behind them which the Bible can offer.

Kenyon in the preface to the work just referred to beautifully expresses the significance of these facts: "The Bible has a twofold history, internal and external. The internal history deals with the character of its narrative and its teaching, as a revelation of God and of

God's will; the external history tells how and when the several books were written, and how they have been preserved to us. The former treats of the Bible in its divine, the latter in its human, aspect. The former is unique, differing not merely in detail, but in kind, from the history of any other book; the latter is shared by the Bible with every other book that ever was written. It is, of course, its internal history which is of supreme value; but the very greatness of this value gives to the external history of the Bible a special interest and importance above that of all other books. If the Bible claims so unparalleled a pre-eminence, it is of the first consequence to us to know when and how it was written, whether the several books of it are authentic, and whether they have been faithfully handed down to us through the centuries which separate us from the time of their origin'' (*ibid.*, p. ii).

Although the transmission of a reliable Scripture tells us nothing of the process of revelation-inspiration per se, it can set our minds at rest that what we read today in a standard version of the Bible is essentially the message as prophet and apostle gave it, despite translations and the tedious copying processes by which it has reached us.

In concluding these twin chapters (6 and 7), which we have suggested should be studied together, let us freely confess that we have by no means resolved the deepest problems in our understanding of revelation-inspiration. But with the help of the writings of Ellen G. White on the subject, we have offered presently available insights that can protect us from positions which have decimated the faith of other Christians in the authority of the Bible.

The following words seem most relevant before we move to the more personal dimensions of our subject: ''This Holy Book has withstood the assaults of Satan, who has united with evil men to make everything of divine character shrouded in clouds and darkness. But the Lord has preserved this Holy Book by His own miraculous power in its present shape—a chart or guidebook to the human family to show them the way to heaven'' (*Selected Messages*, Book One, p. 15).

CHAPTER VIII

GOD SPEAKS TO ME BY HIS SPIRIT

In these days when people cry for relevance, it is a sweet assurance that God speaks to us by His Spirit. Directly, personally. Of course, many who claim such an assurance do not even seriously consider the relevance of a two-thousand-year-old Book. The here-and-now people, the people moved by a "happening"—whatever is happening—often do not take stock in a Book associated with quaint Elizabethan English!

Just to show that this contemporary attitude on the authority of "my personal experience" with the Holy Spirit is not completely the corner of the 1970's, let me relate an experience that came early in my ministry, about thirty years ago. I had been studying the Bible with a deeply interested lady, and she appreciated all that she learned week by week until we came to the Ten Commandments and the Sabbath. Despite my lack of experience, I sensed a reaction like that which must have come from the rich young ruler in Christ's day. Then one evening she brightened. "Look," she said. "I can see from the Bible that the seventh day is the Sabbath. But I believe in the guidance of the Holy Spirit. And when the Spirit wants *me* to keep the seventh day as the Sabbath, He will show it to me personally. Until He does, I cannot move out on the question."

Does not the Holy Spirit guide into all truth? Well, then, how can I do something the Bible requires unless and until the Holy Spirit guides me into seeing and believing that truth?

In looking for answers to these and parallel questions, we must pick our way carefully. Not that the Bible has made the role of the Holy Spirit obscure, but in addition to our own obstructing preconceptions, the Holy Spirit's nature has elements of mystery (in the best sense of that word) associated with it.

If I discover tension or seeming conflict between the guidance which I believe the Holy Spirit is giving me and what the Bible seems to be telling me, then which is normative? In other words, which of these sources takes precedence?

We have to remind ourselves (and perhaps this is the most helpful place to do it) that we are not really describing two independent and separate sources of God's self-revelation. The Spirit whom Jesus promised would guide the church is the same Spirit who inspired the writers of the Bible in the first place. Only our own confused thinking expects tension between the Spirit and the Bible.

The major difference, however, is that the Bible is God's Word to us in black and white. The Spirit has provided it in preparation for the centuries when neither Saviour, prophet, nor apostle would be present among us. The leading of the Spirit, on the other hand, at the level of illumination (as opposed to inspiration in the sense in which prophets and apostles experienced it) is subject to the frailties of our human nature and ever-present biases. This frailty alone requires that the Bible be normative to our personal understanding of the Spirit's leading, for the Spirit will not contradict Himself.

" 'To the law and to the testimony: if they speak not according to this word, it is because there is no light in them' (Isa. 8:20). Even the work of the Holy Spirit upon the heart is to be tested by the Word of God. The Spirit which inspired the Scriptures, always leads to the Scriptures" (*Selected Messages*, Book One, p. 43).

Jesus Himself associated the promised Spirit with the work of leading the church into the truths which Jesus had already taught. " 'I have yet many things to say to you, but you cannot bear them now. When the Spirit of truth comes, he will guide you into all the truth; for he will not speak on his own authority, but whatever he hears he will speak, and he will declare to you the things that are to come. He will glorify me, for he will take what is mine and declare it to you' " (John 16:12-14, RSV).

" 'These things I have spoken to you, while I am still with you. But the Counselor, the Holy Spirit, whom the Father will send in my name, he will teach you all things, and bring to your remembrance all that I have said to you' " (John 14:25, 26, RSV).

Likewise the Spirit bestows His gifts upon the church to build its faith. "And his gifts were that some should be apostles, some prophets, some evangelists, some pastors and teachers, for the equipment of the saints, for the work of ministry, for building up the body of Christ, until we all attain to the unity of the faith and of the knowledge of the Son of God, to mature manhood, to the measure of the stature of the fulness of Christ; so that we may no longer be children, tossed to and fro and carried about with every wind of doctrine, by the cunning of men, by their craftiness in deceitful wiles. Rather, speaking the truth in love, we are to grow up in every way into him who is the head, into Christ, from whom the whole body, joined and knit together by every joint with which it is supplied, when each part is working properly, makes bodily growth and upbuilds itself in love'' (Ephesians 4:11-16, RSV).

The essential harmony between Jesus' teachings and our understanding of these teachings through the Spirit's ministry is clearly indicated in the following inspired words: ''Because of their selfishness and earthliness, even the disciples of Jesus could not comprehend the spiritual glory which He sought to reveal unto them. It was not until after Christ's ascension to His Father, and the outpouring of the Holy Spirit upon the believers, that the disciples fully appreciated the Saviour's character and mission.

''After they had received the baptism of the Spirit, they began to realize that they had been in the very presence of the Lord of glory. As the sayings of Christ were brought to their remembrance, their minds were opened to comprehend the prophecies, and to understand the miracles which He had wrought. . . . The disciples now seemed, to themselves, of much less importance than before they realized this. They never wearied of rehearsing His words and works. His lessons, which they had but dimly understood, now came to them as a fresh revelation. The Scriptures became to them a new book'' (*The Desire of Ages,* pp. 506, 507).

So we return to our need for the Spirit if we are to know and understand truth. Does He raise our IQ's so that we can understand? We recall that He will bring to our remembrance the promises of God's Word when we need them to battle temptation (see John 14:26). He did this work for the apostles when they went out as eyewitnesses of all that Jesus had done and taught. But the Holy Spirit seems to do an even more vital work for us.

Jesus once declared, '' 'My teaching is not mine, but his who sent me; if any man's will is to do his will, he shall know whether the teaching is from God or whether I am speaking on my own authority. He who speaks on his own authority seeks his own glory; but he who seeks the glory of him who sent him is true, and in him there is no falsehood' " (John 7:16-18, RSV). These words indicate that "the perception and appreciation of truth . . . depends less upon the mind than upon the heart. . . . If truth could be submitted to the reason alone, pride would be no hindrance in the way of its reception." And this is where the work of the Holy Spirit comes in. "It is to be received through the work of grace in the heart; and its reception depends upon the renunciation of every sin that the Spirit of God reveals" (*ibid.*, p. 455).

We take pride in our learning and in our degrees, but "man's advantages for obtaining a knowledge of the truth, however great these may be, will prove of no benefit to him unless the heart is open to receive the truth, and there is a conscientious surrender of every habit and practice that is opposed to its principles" (*ibid.,* pp. 455, 456).

Thus a person of humble talents and little training in science, literature, or philosophy, might have a deep understanding of God's Word, because his heart is in tune with the Spirit who inspired the messages in the first place. In fact, human pride, which often motivates and accompanies scholastic achievement, erects one of the greatest barriers to spiritual perception. "He who speaks on his own authority seeks his own glory; but he who seeks the glory of him who sent him is true, and in him there is no falsehood" (John 7:18, RSV).

The one who is "born of the Spirit" will most likely grasp the true meaning of the views of God and mankind which the same Spirit impressed upon the minds of chosen human instruments centuries ago.

Nowhere was the significance of the Spirit's presence and power more evident than at Pentecost, and a definite preparation of heart was prerequisite to the reception of the promised power (see Luke 24:47). When, through the grace of Christ and the preparatory work of the Holy Spirit (see John 20:22), the apostles and disciples were "all together in one place," the promised bestowal came. With the blessing came many gifts of the Spirit—languages, remembrance of Jesus' words, understanding of the meaning of His words, fearlessness, administrative skills, teaching and preaching power, healing, discernment, and whatever else the gospel commission necessitated.

If anything in this account sounds remote and irrelevant to our day, let us remind ourselves that the presence and power of the Spirit will also mark the close of the gospel work. And how much more desperately we need it now in view of life's complexity, the population explosion, the intensity marking our times, and the nagging fear that saps natural courage and optimism. Except for Christ Himself, the Holy Spirit is unquestionably the most vital aspect of God's self-revelation to man. And it is more desirable that He speak to me today when varied voices clamor for my attention than ever before.

Having spoken of the necessity of humility and willingness to do God's will on the part of the one who hopes the Spirit will help him know saving truth in the Word, we must also assert that only he who diligently works the mine of truth will be most rewarded. The Holy Spirit does not give spiritual perception to the dilatory or the indifferent (see *Christ's Object Lessons,* p. 111). "Some think that an education or a thorough knowledge of the Scriptures is of little consequence if only a man has the Spirit. But God never sends His Spirit to sanction ignorance" (*Gospel Workers,* pp. 105, 106).

It may be only an impression without statistical support, but Seventh-day Adventists do not seem to be the people of the Bible that they once were. Why? Surely there is not less evidence of the need for urgency in our preparation for Jesus' coming. There could be a host of reasons for the diminution of deep study of God's Word, but not one should be related to our looking for the Spirit's manifestations among us. Such can never replace the Word of God. We are probably preoccupied with the pressure and pace of life—the steady migration to the cities, the pressure for formal schooling, the mere economic tensions from our heightened expectations—that dominate our time and energies and leave us sapped of the drive to know, to memorize, to comprehend. But the Spirit comes in close association with the Word, and without the Word we could heed a false spirit and not know it.

With the charismatic wave that is sweeping our world today, it is easy for believers to associate the Bible with God's restrictions and laws but to associate the Holy Spirit with a happy flight of freedom and exhilaration. We must constantly relate our Christian experience to the purpose for which Christ came. He came to seek and to save the lost. We are lost in sin. Sin is disharmony with the will, the law, of

God. This was what put us out of harmony with God in the beginning. The whole goal of God's self-revelation is our restoration to harmony with the law which God had engraved on the hearts of our first parents. God has specifically designed the new covenant to rewrite that law in our hearts. And the Spirit has that same goal and purpose.

It is almost beyond our comprehension that we can become partakers of the divine nature and escape the corruption that is in the world through lust (see 2 Peter 1:4). But Christ has appointed His Spirit as the agency for this miracle of divine love. "Sin could be resisted and overcome only through the mighty agency of the Third Person of the Godhead, who would come with no modified energy, but in the fullness of divine power. It is the Spirit that makes effectual what has been wrought out by the world's Redeemer. It is by the Spirit that the heart is made pure. Through the Spirit the believer becomes a partaker of the divine nature. Christ has given His Spirit as a divine power to overcome all hereditary and cultivated tendencies to evil, and to impress His own character upon His church" (*The Desire of Ages,* p. 671).

However, no casual relationship to the Holy Spirit can transform the life and character. "There are many who believe and profess to claim the Lord's promise; they talk about Christ and about the Holy Spirit, yet receive no benefit. They do not surrender the soul to be guided and controlled by the divine agencies. We cannot use the Holy Spirit. The Spirit is to use us. Through the Spirit God works in His people 'to will and to do of His good pleasure.' Phil. 2:13. But many will not submit to this. They want to manage themselves. This is why they do not receive the heavenly gift. Only to those who wait humbly upon God, who watch for His guidance and grace, is the Spirit given. The power of God awaits their demand and reception. This promised blessing, claimed by faith, brings all other blessings in its train. It is given according to the riches of the grace of Christ, and He is ready to supply every soul according to the capacity to receive" (*ibid.,* p. 672).

We need our visions cleared, our faith challenged, our hope reassured so that we can shake off our Laodicean apathy, clear the rubbish from the doorways to our hearts, and welcome the waiting Saviour. "All who consecrate soul, body, and spirit to God will be constantly receiving a new endowment of physical and mental power. The inexhaustible supplies of heaven are at their command. Christ gives them the breath of His own spirit, the life of His own life. The Holy Spirit puts forth its highest energies to work in heart and mind. The grace of God enlarges and multiplies their faculties, and every perfection of the divine nature comes to their assistance in the work of saving souls. Through co-operation with Christ they are complete in Him, and in their human weakness they are enabled to do the deeds of Omnipotence'' (*ibid.*, p. 827).

CHAPTER IX

GOD SPEAKS THROUGH HIS CHURCH

If the Christian church more perfectly reflected the spirit and attitude of the One who said, "I am among you as one who serves" (Luke 22:27, RSV), many more people would feel that God can speak to them through the church. The current negative attitude toward the organized church may reflect the general reaction against authority anywhere and in any form. But the church has manifested authoritarianism rather than the winsomeness of God's love so often and so long that many today give her message no serious, open-minded consideration. Any form of coercion by any part of the church misrepresents God. "In the work of redemption there is no compulsion. No external force is employed. Under the influence of the Spirit of God, man is left free to choose whom he will serve" (*The Desire of Ages,* p. 466).

On the surface of it, such a portrayal of God may seem to contradict the Biblical picture of Him. Many regard the Ten Commandments as severe and prohibitory. For example, one who attended some of our evangelistic services decided that he might as well lie down and die as to become a Christian—no smoking, no drinking, no sensuality, no shows, no gambling. He could see no happiness left. Just one big NO.

It is also interesting to ask which type of earthly government reflects the heavenly. God does not call a town meeting to decide on His laws. How could He? He is God, and we are His creatures. How can we advise Him or put His will to a vote? Because of His transcendence, He must reveal Himself and His will to us. We cannot discover Him. He has existed from all eternity, and the law expresses in a form adapted to our situation His unchangeable nature. Within these understandings, His government is authoritarian. But He *forces* no one to submit to it. Otherwise there would have been no possibility of rebellion.

The people, however, who will share God's throne—His government and His kingdom—will have chosen His way as best. Contrast the prodigal son's attitude to his father's laws before and after he went away. He left home because he felt they were oppressive. He returned of his own accord and gladly put himself under his father's laws again—this time with gratitude and appreciation.

But we must return to the church. What is the church anyway? How would one define it? How and when did it originate? What authority, if any, does it have? Do I really need the church? Does it need me?

Without Christ there would be no church. The church in Old Testament times consisted of those who entered into a covenant with Yahweh (the Angel of the Covenant, Jesus the Christ) and who showed their faith in the coming Redeemer by offering sacrifices and choosing the way of God's commandments. A familial pattern strongly characterized the patriarchal church. A theocracy marked the church from the Exodus forward. Of course, God did not call the core of the Old Testament church to exclusiveness, but rather He called them to be an example to all the peoples living around them. Conceit and exclusiveness—"we are the people"—was a perversion of their call "out."

In the main, however, we associate church with the New Testament and the mission of Jesus Christ. The very word *ekklēsia* in the New Testament carries the literal meaning "that which is called [*kaleō*] out [*ex* or *ek*]." It is tempting to define the church as those whom Christ has called out of the world and into the church, out of darkness and into light. In fairness to the facts, though, the same term applied to any assembly of persons called to attend a meeting. It could as easily be political or commercial as religious. We do find the "called out" concept in such texts as Luke 5:32, 1 Thessalonians 2:12, 2 Timothy 1:9, and especially 1 Peter 2:9.

The kind of call Christ gave to Enoch, Noah, Abram, Jacob, and Israel as a whole He later gave to a handful of men whom He personally chose, and thereby the Christian church was born. "With the calling of John and Andrew and Simon, of Philip and Nathanael, began the foundation of the Christian church" (*ibid.*, p. 141). To this initial group He added others in short order. But when Jesus ordained the Twelve, He took the first step in church organization. Now if Christ called the church into existence, we should find out how our Lord wants us to think and feel toward His church. He claims to be the Head of His church, His body. Therefore, the church is as much a part of Christ as the reader's body is a part of his or her whole person. To despise the church means to despise Christ (Ephesians 4:4-16).

Considering that fallible but redeemed men and women make up the church, it has unbelievable authority. (It would do us an immeasurable amount of good just to bring together all that inspiration has told us about the Twelve. To use an old expression, they were a real bunch of characters. We can find ourselves somewhere among them!) Yet Jesus made His church the arbiter of sin and righteousness in His absence. " 'Whatsoever ye shall bind on earth shall be bound in heaven: and whatsoever ye shall loose on earth shall be loosed in heaven.' You are acting as the ambassadors of heaven, and the issues of your work are for eternity" (*ibid.,* p. 442).

How can such a thing be? If we had implicit confidence in the apostles, how about those that came to believe on Christ through the apostles' word? How about *us*, the church today? Are we worthy of such authority? No. But in discharging it, Christ has not left us alone. "But we are not to bear this great responsibility alone. Wherever His word is obeyed with a sincere heart, there Christ abides. Not only is He present in the assemblies of the church, but wherever disciples, however few, meet in His name, there also He will be. And He says, 'If two of you shall agree on earth as touching anything that they shall ask, it shall be done for them of My Father which is in heaven' " (*ibid.*).

If we could always hold the *authority* of the church in deference to its gospel *commission,* we should have no major difficulty. But when any individual or small group feels endowed with the divine right to move workers around as a chess player moves his pieces, without any consideration of the conscience or the light which the Lord might have given the man who is bearing His burdens in that particular area, then those people have allowed their authority to overshadow their mission as ambassadors of heaven. They have forgotten that the higher their position in the church, the more perfectly Christ calls upon them to represent Him.

"As Christ lived the law in humanity, so we may do if we will take hold of the Strong for strength. But we are not to place the responsibility of our duty upon others, and wait for them to tell us what to do. We cannot depend for counsel upon humanity. The Lord will teach us our duty just as willingly as He will teach somebody else. If we come to Him in faith, He will speak His mysteries to us personally. Our hearts will often burn within us as One draws nigh to commune with us as He did with Enoch. Those who decide to do nothing in any line that will displease God, will know, after presenting their case before Him, just what course to pursue. And they will receive not only wisdom, but strength. Power for obedience, for service, will be imparted to them, as Christ has promised" (*ibid.,* p. 668).

"Do not depend on any erring man to define your duty. . . . [Psalm 22:22-26 quoted]. These scriptures are right to the point. Every church member should understand that God is the one to whom to look for an understanding of individual duty. It is right that brethren counsel together; but when men arrange just what their brethren shall do, let them answer that they have chosen their Lord as their counselor. Those who will humbly seek Him will find His grace sufficient. But when one man allows another to step in between him and the duty that God has pointed out to him, giving to man his confidence and accepting him as guide, then he steps from the true platform to a false and dangerous one. Such a man, instead of growing and developing, will lose his spirituality" (*Testimonies,* Vol. 9, pp. 279, 280).

Christ based the authority of His church upon the authority of the Holy Spirit in her midst, and the test of whether a certain power is of the Holy Spirit or not is found in the authority of the Bible as God's Word and in the inspired understanding of that Word as given through the gift of prophecy. In reality, then, the authority of the church rests not in the men and women called as members of the church nor even in those called to lead the church through various ministries. There is, therefore, no valid basis for pride of office nor an assuming of prerogatives over the lives and souls of others.

On the other hand, it is our duty to show respect for and a willingness to receive counsel from those who faithfully perform the service of their God-appointed office and thus reflect the servant-role exemplified by Jesus Christ. Although the context of the next inspired words is the reception of the gospel message, the principle applies to our attitude toward ministers and teachers, lay pastors and church officers: "We offer insult to the Prince of life, and put Him to shame before the synagogue of Satan and before the heavenly universe when we refuse to listen to His delegated messengers, and instead listen to the agents of Satan, who would draw the soul away from Christ. So long as one does this, he can find no hope or pardon, and he will finally lose all desire to be reconciled to God" (*The Desire of Ages,* p. 325).

Although the church is God's extended family on earth, it is not a closed family that exists for itself alone. Indeed, its function as witness to the power of the gospel provides the reason for the church's existence and authority. Jesus connected the assurance of His closeness to His followers with the commission, "Go! Teach! Disciple! Baptize! And I am with you all the time, everywhere, until the work is done, until the end of the age."

Signs and wonders will follow the believers when they bear witness to Christ, for the Spirit has bestowed His gifts for the successful accomplishment of the church's mission. "Therefore we must pay the closer attention to what we have heard, lest we drift away from it. For if the message declared by angels was valid and every transgression or disobedience received a just retribution, how shall we escape if we neglect such a great salvation? It was declared at first by the Lord, and it was attested to us by *those who heard him,* while God also bore witness by signs and wonders and various miracles and by gifts of the Holy Spirit distributed according to his own will" (Hebrews 2:1-4, RSV, emphasis added).

Think how the disciples of Jesus were behaving just six weeks or so before Pentecost. Is there any limit to what the Holy Spirit can do through a surrendered heart and a Christ-conquered soul, as in Peter's experience?

I believe that the church has lost the respect due to her because, in part at least, she has lost living contact with her Lord. We have heard many times that as love wanes and as the Spirit withdraws, we fill the vacuum with a great bustle of activity and a complexity of organizational machinery until the policy books are never adequate to cover all the angles, and the council agendas overflow with paraphernalia.

God is ready and heaven is impatiently waiting to bestow on the church the same evidences of divine approval and authority that marked the apostolic church. "The promise is as far-reaching as the commission. Not that all the gifts are imparted to each believer. The Spirit divides 'to every man severally as He will.' 1 Cor. 12:11. But the gifts of the Spirit are promised to every believer according to his need for the Lord's work. The promise is just as strong and trustworthy now as in the days of the apostles. 'These signs shall follow them that believe.' This is the privilege of God's children, and faith should lay hold on all that it is possible to have as an indorsement of faith'' (*ibid.,* p. 823).

As a people we have often placed such priority on Bible doctrines and prophecy that we have almost placed an anathema upon the expectation of signs and wonders. (Here is where it is hard for us to keep a balance.) But God plans to give us ''signs'' as ''an *indorsement* of faith''—not as the sole basis of faith (for the devil can match signs), but as a backup, a support, a present evidence that God is working through His church.

I have some medical friends who are earnest, dedicated church members. They believe in prayer, and they believe in anointing. But some of them insist that they have never seen a healing of clinically determined cancer. A non-Adventist doctor has written recently on ''psychic healings.'' A surgeon himself, he subjected himself to psychic surgery and had an ''organ'' removed. He portrays the whole thing as a hoax except that such treatment might help emotionally. Then he declares that a terminal cancer probably can never be cured by divine healing. Let's begin to claim our privileges as God's children and reach out by faith for all that God in His wisdom will give as an endorsement of our faith.

'' 'They shall lay hands on the sick, and they shall recover.' This world is a vast lazar house, but Christ came to heal the sick, to proclaim deliverance to the captives of Satan. He was in Himself health and strength. He imparted His life to the sick, the afflicted, those possessed of demons. He turned away none who came to receive His healing power. He knew that those who petitioned Him for help had brought disease upon themselves; yet He did not refuse to heal them. And when virtue from Christ entered into these poor souls, they were convicted of sin, and many were healed of their spiritual disease, as well as of their physical maladies. *The gospel still possesses the same power,* and why should we not today witness the same results?'' (*ibid.,* italics supplied).

It's true that the devil has multiplied his counterfeits, and it's true that we should prevent sickness by teaching healthful living, but it is also true that many by heredity and a life of indulgence have little resource left. Like the man let down through the roof, they may desire healing from oppressive guilt more than physical healing, but some of them can have both blessings—healing of soul and body. God is willing. "He is just as willing to heal the sick now as when He was personally on earth. Christ's servants are His representatives, the channels for His working. He desires through them to exercise His healing power" (*ibid.,* pp. 823, 824).

That means us. That's the church, and if we could more clearly reflect Him whose name we bear, we would see more of His power. People would soon learn that God is with His church. Not all the sick would be healed. We would not start to take the place of God, nor pretend to have His infinite knowledge. We would still have to submit to the will of Him who wants only the best for each of us (see *The Ministry of Healing,* pp. 225-233, "Prayer for the Sick"). But the best for the church is just ahead, as well as an unbelievably terrible testing. "The power of love was in all Christ's healing, and only by partaking of that love, through faith, can we be instruments for His work. If we neglect to link ourselves in divine connection with Christ, the current of life-giving energy cannot flow in rich streams from us to the people. There were places where the Saviour Himself could not do many mighty works because of their unbelief. So now unbelief separates *the church* from her divine Helper. Her hold upon eternal realities is weak. By her lack of faith, God is disappointed, and robbed of His glory" (*The Desire of Ages,* p. 825, italics supplied).

Think of it. Our unbelief robs God of His rightful glory. We have failed to reflect His character, and people inside and outside the church are being turned off. But if we know enough to be in the church—and we are in it now—we have no excuse. We know enough about Him to trust Him if we want to. Why don't we go to work for Him today?

"It is in doing Christ's work that *the church* has the promise of His presence. . . . The very life of *the church* depends upon her faithfulness in fulfilling the Lord's commission. . . . Where there is no active labor for others, love wanes, and faith grows dim" (*ibid.,* italics supplied).

Did we ever wonder who suffers the wrath of the Lamb? It is against those who claim fellowship with Christ and His church, yet they have ignored the needs of their fellowmen. "The sufferings of every man are the sufferings of God's child, and those who reach out no helping hand to their perishing fellow beings provoke His righteous anger. . . . To those . . . He will declare in the great judgment day, 'I know you not whence ye are; depart from Me, all ye workers of iniquity.' Luke 13:27" *(ibid.)*.

CHAPTER X

GOD SPEAKS THROUGH THE SPIRIT OF PROPHECY

Making the gospel meaningful to our modern world greatly concerns those interested in the speedy completion of the gospel mission. For one thing, many feel that the archaic language of the Bible turns off the modern mind. Along with this accusation many claim that the gospel and the Bible are not relevant to the kind of world we live in today.

We spoke earlier about the value of identifying an accurate text of the Bible (see Chapter 6), and we can gain much from the various revised versions or translations (not paraphrases)—especially those produced by a committee of scholars rather than an individual. But Seventh-day Adventists have an immeasurable advantage in the matter of understanding God's self-revelation.

Through the writings of Ellen G. White, we have God's special messages to this people given in a modern, Indo-European language and in a form of that language only seventy to one hundred years removed from our own day. Since these messages come through a Western culture, we do not have the same major problems of interpretation due to the cultural or linguistic gaps between our world and that of God's ancient people.

As an inspired commentator, Ellen G. White brings out some of the deeper or hidden meanings of Scripture and shows correlations between various passages. Also, the insights from the close parallel between the experience of the Biblical writers and that of Ellen White offer great insight into the revelation-inspiration process through which Scripture has come to us.

In calling attention to this parallel, we recogize that not all church members have had an equal opportunity to test and experience this modern gift of prophecy. Many do not yet have Ellen G. White's books and articles available in their own language, and so they have no exposure at all or perhaps very little. When we remind ourselves that we have a heritage of 100,000 pages of material, we can understand what a tiny proportion of the whole is available in many countries.

Then, too, we must face the differences in culture from country to country. Some, for example, assume most sincerely that Ellen White wrote only to her own people in the United States. However, when they investigate her inspirational books, they see that the objection scarcely applies. So they sometimes will say Yes to *Steps to Christ, The Desire of Ages,* and the like, but No to the *Testimonies for the Church* and other books dealing with such issues as health reform and church standards.

We are grateful for the recent assistance overseas fields are receiving for the translation of the Ellen G. White books into various languages. These countries have taken hold of this program, and many want to learn of the Spirit's special counsels for this church.

All need patience and understanding. Those who have had a long experience with this gift in the church should try to graciously understand those to whom it is new. And those who cannot yet see how God could have chosen to speak to His people in this manner would do well to exercise tolerance toward the enthusiasm of those who are already convinced.

A study of denominational history demonstrates that without the gift of prophecy in our midst from the inception of the movement, Adventism would not exist as we know it today.

Following the traumatic and shattering experience of the great disappointment when the Lord did not return on October 22, 1844, the loose-knit Millerite movement nearly disintegrated overnight. Those who accepted the visions, which first came in December, 1844, had something to keep them from rashness and to keep them prayerfully studying the prophecies. Also to some degree the visions endorsed the various elements of truth which began to fall into place.

Then elements of fanaticism broke out—fanaticism that would have discouraged serious minds from even considering the explanation of the disappointment and the progressive "present truth." So God asked Ellen White to travel among these "torn and peeled" groups, to rebuke fanaticism openly, and to encourage believers in the third angel's message.

Almost every advance move made by the scattered remnant resulted from either the endorsement or the initiative of messages through this frail little person. Church schools, training for ministers, presses to print papers and books, health clinics and treatment rooms to treat and to teach the sick, health food factories, missions to the lands beyond—these and a host of other activities, organizations, and enterprises God fostered through Ellen G. White.

As in apostolic times, the gift appeared in a person who could be seen and heard; but as time went on and the movement grew and the future need of a growing church came into focus, this unlettered woman handwrote thousands of pages of counsel. Ellen G. White regarded her counsel as adequate to take the church into the kingdom, and she had no clear indication of the need for a second messenger.

How many have ever written one hundred pages about anything, let alone 100,000? No wonder Ellen G. White spoke of awakening in the early hours of the morning and of her pen moving across the paper as fast as her hand could direct it.

Then consider the quality, depth, practicality, balance, and tenderness of her messages. Oh, yes, the thunders of Sinai could be heard when the church or individuals refused to heed God's counsel. But what tenderness she could express to the discouraged and depressed! God knew, for example, that some of us feel too sick to think or pray. At such times, she suggested, just rest in Christ's arms (see *The Ministry of Healing,* p. 251).

These are just a few of the basic reasons why this writer believes that God speaks to us through the spirit of prophecy. Some object to the application of Revelation 12:17 and 19:10 to the work of Ellen G. White. They feel sure that the "testimony of Jesus Christ" which is "the spirit of prophecy" means something much broader and more general than the work of one person. And no doubt both expressions can apply to the revelation-inspiration processes by which God revealed Himself in the Bible.

Further, the revised versions do not always give the same expression in Revelation 12:17 as in 19:10, but in the original, the "testimony of Jesus" expression is the same in both verses. Although the expression can be equally translated "testimony" borne by Christians *about* Jesus rather than "testimony" that originates *with* Jesus and is shared through His prophets, Revelation 19:10 specifically ties the testimony or witness to the spirit of prophecy, which inspired all Bible writers. The "remnant" John refers to have the identification mark of the gift of prophecy down at the end-time. In the parallel passage of Revelation 22:9, the brethren who have the testimony of Jesus are also called "the prophets."

When we say that God speaks through the writings of Ellen G. White, we are not thinking only of the Ellen G. White messages to the church at large or to those outside the ranks of the church whom she often addressed. We are thinking of the way in which He reveals Himself to each individual reader, for we find that those who love the spirit of prophecy most have many favorite passages which speak to them in a special way or which met their need in a particular crisis.

There really are few facets of life to which Ellen G. White does not speak. And that again is God speaking, for He is interested in the little things as well as the larger things of our experience.

Apart from the Bible, no writings anywhere do more to uplift Him who said, "And I, when I am lifted up from the earth, will draw all men to myself" (John 12:32, RSV), than do the writings of Ellen G. White. At the same time none more highly exalt God's commandments and character, maintaining a sound and practical balance between the law and the gospel. In fact, on this matter of balance and discernment, my theologian friends describe their amazement at the way in which Ellen White (unschooled in theology) safely worked through the most knotty theological problems.

Now, as this book has progressed, we have quoted more and more from Ellen White. Two factors lie behind this. The first is that we would scarcely dare to say some of the things she has said, so we prefer to let her reprove us or stretch our faith. The second factor is one which a colleague expressed at a Bible conference in 1974. In his presentation on the role of the Holy Spirit in the interpretation of Scripture, he said that he had read all the books available to him on the subject, but when he got through, nothing compared with the help given by Ellen G. White.

Really, when you have an inspired commentary and you believe in it, it is difficult to quote an uninspired source. We do not mean to disparage in any way the use of other sources, but in this book, which deals specifically with the area of revelation-inspiration, we especially need the most authoritative data available.

Finally, I personally question anyone's right to counteract or diminish the distinction which Ellen White made between her writings and the Scriptures. (Some wish to attribute the distinction to her modesty, but can anyone discern motive?) When Ellen White makes the Bible normative to her writings and urges us to test them by the Bible, then if we respect her gift and calling, we should do nothing to modify this relationship.

If we wish, let us say that her writings have supreme authority with us, next to the Bible, but let us not by human reason and uninspired wisdom give her writings an equal authority with Scripture. Too often in our exegesis, preaching, teaching, and writing, we give lip service to the Bible's supremacy, but our actions and general practice declare differently. For too many, the finding of an appropriate Ellen G. White quotation ends all Biblical investigation, exegesis, and use of the many excellent aids to Bible study.

Speaking of exegesis reminds us that the concern of the next chapter is how to interpret what God says—for interpret we all do!

CHAPTER XI

GOD SPEAKS: I UNDERSTAND

Occasionally we meet someone who feels sure that a certain passage of Scripture actually has the meaning which he sees in it and that it can have no other. Likewise, he cannot understand why everybody else cannot see it his way.

In receiving the inspired messages of the Bible and the writings of Ellen G. White, we must face the fact that everyone is very much an individual in the way he understands the messages. This is not due to the uniqueness of *inspired* messages as distinct from other messages. It simply follows from the facts of the communication process. Put it in the familiar words of communicators: "Meaning is not in words. Meaning is in people using the words and in people receiving the words."

In a theoretical sense, all communication involves the receiver's interpretation. Fortunately, in everyday living our vocabulary and rhetoric overlap so largely that for all practical purposes we experience little or no breakdown in communication. But the more technical, the more specialized, the more distinctive from routine the message is, the greater the likelihood that the individuality of interpretation will exist.

If communication is the transfer of meaning from one individual to another, it is possible that the recipient of the message will not take from the communication channel exactly the same message that the sender put in. To state the matter another way, the more exactly the source's encoding capacity matches the receiver's decoding capacity, the greater the likelihood of a close similarity between the message sent and the message received.

We live some two thousand years later than the last Biblical writers. Theirs was a Hebrew-Jewish culture in the main, although they had begun to move toward the Gentile world and were influenced by Greek culture in some areas. We have no autograph (an original) of any single book, chapter, or even verse of the Bible. The languages in which the inspired writers worked are not our modern languages. So we face the complications to effective communication which translation always creates. Again, we have largely become urban people today, whereas the Biblical scene was basically rural. These are all factors of difference between the source (Biblical writers) and the present receivers (ourselves).

When Jesus was here, He interpreted the Old Testament to His disciples. The classic example occurred on the famous walk to Emmaus (Luke 24:27). We refer to it particularly because the word *diērmēneusen* appears in the Greek text. From it we have taken our English word *hermeneutics,* or the science of interpretation. Now why did Jesus need to "hermeneut" the Old Testament for the disciples? Because of their expectations, they could not accept Christ's predictions about Himself nor even the reports from their own group that His predictions were dramatically being fulfilled that very day. In order to break the gloom created by their unbelief and to confirm the normative role of Scripture, Jesus, in the guise of a stranger, explained the Scriptures which He had perfectly fulfilled that very weekend. As with them, so with us. Our unbelief and false expectations often distort our interpretation of the Bible and the spirit of prophecy.

The Gospels also reveal that Christ had almost a running debate with the religious leaders over their interpretation of the Old Testament. They looked through such filters as strong nationalism, pride of spiritual ancestry, bitter resentment of their political subservience to Rome, the rabbinical system of tradition, and their confidence in outward form and mental assent as fulfilling Jehovah's will. We share some of the same hindrances to sound interpretation, apart from those which result from the passage of time between us and the last Bible writer. Hebrew thought patterns differed from Greek, and we are oriented toward the latter rather than the former. Yet even Peter, Paul's contemporary, intimates a problem in correctly interpreting some of Paul's writing (2 Peter 3:15, 16).

Once we accept the need for sound hermeneutics, we would do well to list our objectives in interpretation. Since the Bible writers wrote and spoke to their contemporaries, we should discover first what they were saying to their own times and people. This is the basic objective. We should next ask if the passing of time and the appearance of later inspired writings add meanings to the original intent which the author may or may not have foreseen, yet which the Spirit had foreknown. Then there is the additional goal of transmitting the "rightly divided" Word to those of one's own time (2 Timothy 2:15).

We refer the reader to chapters 6 and 7 for a limited consideration of the processes of revelation-inspiration which give the Bible its authority and its right to be its own interpreter. This principle underlies all sound interpretation or understanding. We have denied the right of other disciplines or fields of knowledge to serve as judges of the Bible (see Chapter 3).

The careful interpreter who respects the Bible's unique character will ever keep in mind the Divine Author behind the whole, although God chose more than a score of different writers as the channels for His self-revelation. So as he studies a specific passage, he compares it with all other passages treating the same subject before he draws firm conclusions as to its meaning.

The unity of the Old and New Testaments affords the key to the Bible's general unity, and the coming of the Messiah is the pivotal point upon which the two Testaments balance. Furthermore, the ongoing unity of Biblical history and the underlying thread of salvific truth in God's self-revelation tie the whole together. The entire Bible provides the ultimate context for understanding any part of it despite the diversity of the writers and the stretch of years during which they wrote.

While we should fully draw upon every field of knowledge that can enrich our understanding of the two Testaments—fields like archaeology, linguistics, comparative religions, the sciences, philosophy, extra-Biblical religion, Hebrew or ecclesiastical traditions—we must not permit any of these to set the norm for understanding the Bible.

We have referred to the thread of spiritual truth that runs through God's Word. But we must stress that an individual's willingness to receive and be molded by spiritual truth—made tangible, living, and personal in Jesus Christ—primarily determines his capacity to understand truth (John 7:16, 17).

But what shall we do when equally sincere believers form different conclusions in their understanding of the same Scriptural passages? Shall we turn our heads and hope that the differences will go away? Shall we open up debate and declare with seeming magnanimity, "May the best man win" (suspecting, of course, that we are "the best")? Shall we search out sympathizers so that we can say, "More are following me"? Really, what course should we take?

It would be ideal and most helpful if both parties could maintain absolute objectivity. Each would study, think, and write as though he were completely unconcerned as to whether his view or another should prevail. Each party would be dedicated solely to the pursuit of truth (the goal and sometimes claimed posture of learning in every field). But absolute objectivity is an unrealized and probably unrealizable ideal. A few might reach it occasionally about some things, but consistently—hardly. So what to do?

The first line of defense against subjectivity is to constantly acknowledge its strong and frequent occurrence. We should also remember Jesus' prayer for "those who believe in me through their word . . . that they may all be one; even as thou, Father, art in me, and I in thee, that they also may be in us" (John 17:20, 21). When each student of the Word feels more anxious to retain his brother's love than to win an argument, there would be some basis for disagreeing agreeably. One also needs to consider on what levels of truth he should take a Martin Luther position: " 'Here I stand, I can do no other; may God help me.' "

Certainly we cannot compromise the clearly defined, known will of God when the position has been patiently studied and presented with sufficient time to ascertain that those involved understand the issues. But often we ardently differ over what Ellen White has called "unsettled questions"—unessential to salvation and not central in God's self-revelation (see *Evangelism,* pp. 154, 155, 183; *Testimonies,* Vol. 4, pp. 65, 66). Our contentions often arise from our attempts to explain what God has called "a mystery."

One Adventist began explaining the mystery of godliness, God with us, God manifest in the flesh. Ellen G. White told him that the mystery remained just as great after his explanations as before (*Selected Messages,* Book One, p. 177). She also indicated that not everybody would see the new birth, or the grace of Christ, or the operations of the Holy Spirit from exactly the same viewpoint (*ibid.*, pp. 177, 183). She pleaded to leave room for the Lord "to work upon the mind, to speak to the soul, and to impress the understanding." None were to take sides or make divisions—even over such crucial matters.

"Then," says one, "is nothing certain? Is everything up for sale?" No, but within the body of the saints we need to reconcile our differences and to seek unity within our diversities.

"Well, then," reasons another, "why can't I believe anything I like and remain a Seventh-day Adventist? My friends are all in the church. My family is in the church. Just make the circle wide enough to take me in. Why try to push anyone out?"

This proposal has much to commend it provided that no one uses it as a Trojan horse to undermine the church's security. It is one thing to perceive a basic truth from a slightly varying viewpoint. It is something else altogether to make science, philosophy, contemporary religions, reason, or ecclesiastical councils determine the meaning of the Bible. When the *foundation* of Scriptural authority is either deliberately or unintentionally undermined, there is neither space nor time for compromise. There can be no unity there. Drawing the circle wide enough to take in such principles of interpretation would leave no circle!

Chapter 22 of *Selected Messages,* Book One, separates those things that we should dwell upon from those which we should not. Nearly ninety years ago Ellen G. White predicted the exact issue facing our church today. "But God will have a people upon the earth to maintain the Bible, and the Bible only, as the standard of all doctrines and the basis of all reforms. The opinions of learned men, the deductions of science, the creeds or decisions of ecclesiastical councils, as numerous and discordant as are the churches which they represent, the voice of the majority—not one nor all of these should be regarded as evidence for or against any point of religious faith. Before accepting any doctrine or precept, we should demand a plain 'Thus saith the Lord' in its support" (*The Great Controversy,* p. 595).

That statement clearly declares the *sola scriptura* principle and delineates some of the most persistent and effective underminers of Biblical authority in the world today. God's servant foresaw a people who would champion the Bible's authority above all other authorities.

Each of us must determine, as God speaks to us, on what basis and by what principles we will interpret His Word. In turn, our understanding will govern how we respond—the next vital step in the communication process.

The issue is of utmost importance because our eternal salvation could be at stake. Sincerity in believing error will not necessarily excuse us in God's sight.

Chapter XII

GOD SPEAKS: I RESPOND

Communication theory suggests that no communication is complete until the source of the message has experienced the response of the receiver. In fact, communications people think of communication as an ongoing cycle that operates just as soon as two communicating units come within communicating distance. The receiver could just as readily be thought of as the source and the source as the receiver, but for the convenience of discussion, and to distinguish the response from the message, it is spoken of as "feedback."

Now with God communication is quite different than it is with us because, for one thing, He does not have to await our overt feedback signals in order to get our response. In His omniscience, He can read our minds, thoughts, and physiological responses to all the stimuli that reach us. But our intelligent and willful response to His specific self-revelation particularly interests Him. He watches with great longing for us to respond with love to His self-revelation.

Have you observed a mother watching for the first signal of response from her baby? It may be a fleeting, "burpy" smile, but oh how she treasures it. Can we imagine that God watches us like that for a sign of our response? "Our Redeemer thirsts for recognition. He hungers for the sympathy and love of those whom He has purchased with His own blood. He longs with inexpressible desire that they should come to Him and have life. *As the mother watches for the smile of recognition from her little child,* which tells of the dawning of intelligence, so does Christ watch for the expression of grateful love, which shows that spiritual life is begun in the soul" (*The Desire of Ages,* p. 191, italics supplied).

If we could only let our faith grasp the assurance of God's loving care and personal interest in us no matter what or who we are, it would change our outlook on life. Loneliness, feeling unwanted or unappreciated, would surely disappear, and we would certainly praise God more than we do now.

Praise and worship express genuine, heartfelt response to God's revelation of Himself. True worship leaves no room for display or competition. "But the hour is coming, and now is, when the true worshipers will worship the Father in spirit and truth, for such the Father seeks to worship him. God is spirit, and those who worship him must worship in spirit and truth" (John 4:23, 24, RSV).

Furthermore, true worship implies obedience. Indeed, the supreme form of worship is obedience, which reminds us of the two boys whose father asked them to work in his vineyard. The one gave lip service in a respectful (worshipful) way when he simply stated, "I am on my way, sir." But like boys and girls playing hooky from school, he found a diversion on the way. The other brashly refused to go but repented of his waywardness and actually went. There could have been two other possibilities in the story—a boy who would say, "I go," and really would, and a boy who would say, "I am not going," and really would not. Perhaps there could have been yet one more category—a boy who would not respond at all to his father's command. He could be as one who had not heard.

We might fool a human father by our responses, but not the Reader of hearts. Men deceive themselves into believing that they have no obligation to respond to God or that if they ignore His voice He will not hold them accountable for a response or its absence. God has the ultimate word for each. "There are only two classes in the world today, and only two classes will be recognized in the judgment—those who violate God's law and those who obey it. Christ gives the test by which to prove our loyalty or disloyalty. 'If ye love Me,' He says, 'keep My commandments' " (*Christ's Object Lessons,* p. 283).

So in the sinner's response to the holy and righteous God, the crucial test is obedience *now,* not just before the gates of heaven open. Those entrusted with the unfettered freedom of heaven will need to have made obedience a habit. Why, then, do we study God's Word and the writings of Ellen G. White? In order to know more perfectly what He would have us to do, and we can strengthen our wills by strengthening the faith that works by love.

Love is very much at the heart of response to God, because it is the only positive response to Him who personifies love and who constantly pours out perfect love to all His creation. Love awakens love (see *The Desire of Ages,* p. 22). It is the culture in which the human heart thrives. God's love seeks us out and constantly endeavors to restore in us the love that was ours when He made us in His image.

It is difficult to talk about faith or obedience without being misunderstood or misinterpreted. When we urge obedience as the proper response to God, many cry, "Legalism." Let us face facts. We lost Eden by disobedience. Would anyone dispute that? The eternal character of heaven is harmony with God's perfect will, and that harmony results from obedience. The angels were shocked to discover that they were under a law, because they had been so happy in their perfect response to God's love that they had no sense of bondage.

"But in heaven, service is not rendered in the spirit of legality. When Satan rebelled against the law of Jehovah, the thought that there was a law came to the angels almost as an awakening to something unthought of. In their ministry the angels are not as servants, but as sons. There is perfect unity between them and their Creator. Obedience is to them no drudgery. Love for God makes their service a joy. So in every soul wherein Christ, the hope of glory, dwells, His words are re-echoed, 'I delight to do Thy will, O My God: yea, Thy law is within My heart.' (Psalm 40:8)" (*Thoughts From the Mount of Blessing,* p. 109).

Some scarcely want to believe that the angels are under law or ever were for fear that they, too, will be in a legalistic situation. But please notice: "The will of God is expressed in the precepts of His holy law, and the principles of this law are the principles of heaven. The angels of heaven attain unto no higher knowledge than to know the will of God, and to do His will is the highest service that can engage their powers. But in heaven, service is not rendered in the spirit of legality" *(ibid.).*

If the angels find their highest joy in obeying God's holy law without falling into legalism, is not the same possibility open to us? Obedience can become legalism only when I think that my obedience might make me worthy of salvation, might earn it for me, or at least build merit toward it. Legalism threatens if I think and act as though I could obey by my own power and because of my good nature. But when in dependence upon God I obey the revelation of His love, there is no legalistic base in it. When we mention "union" and "dependence" in connection with the believer's relationship to Christ, I recall His illustration of the vine in John 15:1-17. As I have studied it with the aid of *The Desire of Ages,* pages 674-677, I find the following kinds of assurance in it.

We can no more obey God than a branch severed from a vine can bear fruit. When the cross of Calvary makes us aware that as branches of the wild vine of sinful humanity we can never bear fruit for God's kingdom, we become willing to allow the Divine Vinedresser to sever us from the wild vine and to graft us into the True Vine.

By virtue of the wounds which Christ received for us, we can be grafted in through faith and surrender to Him. The Father carefully tends this union as "fiber by fiber, vein by vein" the new branch grows into the vine stock. "The life of the vine becomes the life of the branch." And all that the branch inherently lacks, the True Vine provides by His victory in our nature. So the branch is treated as Christ deserves, because Christ was willing to be treated as the branch deserved. Christ was condemned for the sin of the branch in which He had no share, in order that the branch might be justified by Christ's righteousness, in which the branch had no share. Christ suffered the death due the branch in order that the branch might receive the life which was His. With the stripes of Christ, the branch is healed (see *ibid.,* p. 25).

"By faith in Him as a personal Saviour the union is formed. The sinner unites his weakness to Christ's strength, his emptiness to Christ's fullness, his frailty to Christ's enduring might. Then he has the mind of Christ. The humanity of Christ has touched our humanity, and our humanity has touched divinity. Thus through the agency of the Holy Spirit man becomes a partaker of the divine nature. He is accepted in the Beloved" (*ibid.,* p. 675).

Perhaps many (especially under the impact of the various "Jesus movements") think of response as a one-time thing. However, the key word in Jesus' object lesson of the vine is *abide,* which makes the symbol of the vine very beautiful and vital. If we rightly understand and transcribe into living experience the word *abide,* we need not fear an unfinished work of grace in our lives when Jesus comes. Permanence characterizes the union of the branch with the vine. Branches do not jump away from trees and try to go it alone! Rightly understood, abiding is the only requirement of the branch once the grafting has taken place.

Furthermore, the vine also lives in the branch. " 'He who abides in me, and I in him, he it is that bears much fruit, for apart from me you can do nothing' " (John 15:5, RSV). But *how?* "It is through the word that Christ abides in His followers. This is the same vital union that is represented by eating His flesh and drinking His blood. The words of Christ are spirit and life. Receiving them, you receive the life of the Vine. . . . Living in Christ, . . . supported by Christ, drawing nourishment from Christ, you bear fruit after the similitude of Christ" (*ibid.,* p. 677).

Jesus represents no casual on-again, off-again connection with Christ, and He undertakes all if the branch will only abide. The Vinedresser does not compel the branch to abide; otherwise Christ would not repeatedly urge that it should abide and would not warn of dread consequences for not abiding. But if the branch will constantly *choose* to abide, no one can force it from its place. It alone governs whether it will abide or not.

Above all else, God wants us to choose to abide in Jesus. "For by grace you have been saved through faith; and this is not your own doing, it is the gift of God—not because of works, lest any man should boast. For we are his workmanship, created in Christ Jesus for good works, which God prepared beforehand, that we should walk in them" (Ephesians 2:8-10, RSV).

"As therefore you received Christ Jesus the Lord, so live in him, rooted and built up in him and established in the faith, just as you were taught, abounding in thanksgiving" (Colossians 2:6, 7, RSV).

Should we worry about our fruit-bearing, whether it is enough, satisfactory, adequate, pleasing? Not if we are abiding. Although the Vinedresser has a knife and uses it, He does not cut off the branches unless they make that choice themselves (John 15:6). For what purpose, then, is the knife? "Every branch that does bear fruit he prunes, that it may bear more fruit" (v. 2, RSV). If the branch continually chooses to abide, the Father takes the responsibility for the fruitfulness of the branch.

"From the chosen twelve who had followed Jesus, one as a withered branch was about to be taken away; the rest were to pass under the pruning knife of bitter trial. Jesus with solemn tenderness explained the purpose of the husbandman. The pruning will cause pain, but it is the Father who applies the knife. He works with no wanton hand or indifferent heart. There are branches trailing upon the ground; these must be cut loose from the earthly supports to which their tendrils are fastening. They are to reach heavenward, and find their support in God. The excessive foliage that draws away the life current from the fruit must be pruned off. The overgrowth must be cut out, to give room for the healing beams of the Sun of Righteousness. The husbandman prunes away the harmful growth, that the fruit may be richer and more abundant'' (*ibid.,* pp. 676, 677).

Thinking back to the role of the Word in the abiding experience, can we not see what a devastating blow the enemy of God and man has struck by undermining the church's confidence in the authority of Christ's words in suggesting that we do not really have His words but only those which the church later thought He should say? So she selected and edited from various traditions that which would help her own situation. One encouraging thing is that some of the most recent scholarly works express confidence in the veracity of the history found in both Testaments. ''It is through the word that Christ abides in His followers.''

I have heard people ask, ''Why does not God *force* me to believe? Why doesn't He send lightning down to touch me and say—'You! I am speaking to you! Now come, before it is too late!'' They desire some kind of overwhelming evidence that would leave no room whatever for unbelief.

One day God will provide overwhelming evidence, as when the first raindrops fell on Noah's ark, but please note, no one got into the ark after that! The panorama of the ages will sweep before the arrested eyes of the inhabitants of earth, and when the evidence is all in, not one voice will protest. The cross of Calvary will silence every complaint, and every knee will bow and every tongue confess the righteousness of God in all His dealings. Even the first complainer will remain defenseless when the panorama of the ages has swept by.

Yet can we call that a response to God's self-revelation? It will be a response of a kind, but it will have no salvation in it. It will be the kind of response wrung from Pharaoh or Balaam. If the heart is not with it, a mental response is not adequate. A response with salvation in it must spring from faith which works by love and purifies the soul.

Calvary and Gethsemane and Sinai still reveal God's character of love. We will never know completely the length and breadth, the depth and height of His love, for it lies beyond us always—like the vast oceans. But come to Gethsemane, where the down-steppingness of God reached the depths of depths. "Christ was now standing in a different attitude from that in which He had ever stood before. His suffering can best be described in the words of the prophet, 'Awake, O Sword, against My shepherd, and against the man that is My fellow, saith the Lord of hosts.' Zech. 13:7. As the substitute and surety for sinful man, Christ was suffering under divine justice. He saw what justice meant. Hitherto He had been as an intercessor for others; now He longed to have an intercessor for Himself" (*ibid.*, p. 686).

Stay with Him in Gethsemane, but do not sleep as did the disciples. Contemplate the agony of Father, Son, and Holy Spirit. Hear Christ's bitter cry for deliverance from drinking the thrice-proffered cup. But He did drink. He drank it for you, for me. He drank it that soon He might speak with us face-to-face.

CHAPTER XIII

GOD WILL SPEAK TO ME FACE-TO-FACE

God has spoken! We say it now on the basis of His revelations through the various channels we have considered in this book. But the reception of every one of these revelations has required faith. As we saw in the previous chapter, God has not yet provided overwhelming, compelling evidence of Himself. He offers sufficient evidence for faith, but the possibility for doubt He has not yet removed. It takes an active, conscious choice on our part to believe. Gethsemane and Calvary have their strong appeal, but even they are not overwhelming.

Many who actually saw Christ on the cross determined to reject Him or confirmed their earlier decision to reject Him. Their own reasoning power seemed brilliant as they saw Him helpless on the cross. "If He was really God, would He be nailed to a cross?" they reasoned. "In fact, if He *is* God, let Him come down off the cross, and we will believe Him!" But would they? Would *that* miracle have offered compelling evidence? What about the raising of Lazarus, whose body had begun to decompose (according to his sister's knowledge of how long he had been dead and the burial practices of their community)?

No, God can accept the love and loyalty of only those who choose to believe on the basis of the loving character they see in His self-revelations. The opportunity to choose, however, will not be ours forever. One day the faith of believers will turn into sight, and the unbelief of doubters will turn into belief through sight. But love will not produce or result from that belated belief, any more than the devils love God, although they believe Him to be exactly who He tells us that He is.

Faith for the devils results in fear. They know the facts. Their knowledge of God predates Eden, when sin dropped a veil between

God and man. Since then God has mercifully denied face-to-face communion. But the devils remember how they worshiped God as they assembled in His presence and did His bidding.

Since sin entered, man has not seen God face-to-face. And the greater the distance from Eden, in one sense, the greater has been man's need for faith. Adam and Eve remembered their face-to-face acquaintance with God, and they often repeated their pre-sin experience to the generations of their children. But by the days of Enoch, men wondered if the old stories were really true. Yet Enoch walked in such close relationship with God that God took him to be with Him and to see Him, presumably face-to-face! Enoch's translation reassured those watching for the Promised Seed of the woman and the fulfillment of the redemption promises. The pledge had been received. There had been an advance payment on the promises of Heaven!

So faith is a very vital ingredient, and it is as much choice and submission to God's will as it is confidence that He is. It expresses the conviction that God has done all things well, that the Judge of all the earth shall do right, and that all things work together for good to them that love the Lord. It means casting all our cares upon Him, because He cares for us.

We cannot explain with our limited knowledge a host of things about God's dealings. When I served on academy and college faculties, we often would say, "Well, if we could just reveal all that we know of the situation, the students would understand why we have done it this way." Often we kept some things to ourselves because we did not wish to expose a student or his family to shame. "In time," we said, "it may get known from other quarters, and then they will understand."

The day will come, however, when "the ills we see, the mysteries of sorrow deep and long," and "the dark enigmas of permitted wrong" will be plain and clear. But now is not the time. Now is the opportunity to develop a faith that trusts and obeys without having all the answers, without having all the whys and wherefores explained, without being able to see the justice of all that happens. Behind the apparent phenomena of good or bad luck we will ultimately see the overruling providences of Him who from His calm eternity ordains that which His providence sees to be best.

Some recent offers by mail have intrigued me. These offers insist that the proffered book or correspondence course will bring me untold wealth and power. People will do what I want them to do without knowing me or knowing why. They will bring me their wealth and count it a privilege. Beautiful and charming women will find my personality irresistible. I can change world events without anyone's knowing it. If that does not echo the voice of one who said, " 'I will exalt . . . [myself]. I will be like the Most High,' " then I do not understand language.

The devil still offers men "the kingdoms of this world" if they will just bow down to him. But the devil does not have all the answers. The psychics and mediums offer only a percentage of right answers and solid predictions. We must never forget the destiny of King Saul when he took the desperate road to the witch of Endor!

One aspect of God's self-revelation we have said little about in this book—His knowledge of the end from the beginning and the accuracy of His predictive prophecies. It may not always be simple to interpret prophecy when conditional factors have to be included. But we do have the more sure word of prophecy. Yet will Adventists succeed in making a fast preparation for the latter rain when the Sunday laws come, when pestilence and famine and earthquake devastate the great cities of the earth? Might that be too late? Why not heed the signals we already have and the prophecies already fulfilled? Perhaps we can be a part of the fulfillment of a known prophecy and yet not recognize our own role.

Or suppose someone really convinced the scientific world that he had discovered the remains of Noah's ark. What would that do to men's faith? What if someone recovered the ark of the covenant? What would that do? Suppose a laboratory of international repute demonstrated scientifically that the rocky foundations of this earth's crust are only six thousand years old. What would that do to men's faith? What if UFO's should be linked in some way with the expected efforts of the devil to portray himself as a healer and benefactor of the world? What would such things do? Would they lead a lot of modern Pharaohs to say, "That's enough. I believe it all now. I'm ready to prepare myself for Christ's kingdom"? Most likely they would change their mind again after the evidence faded.

Belief is simple only for those who, as little children, believe, trust, and obey Him, not because they can prove everything but because He asks them to believe. And He asks us by the various channels of His self-revelation, including the inner witness of His Spirit, who seals our faith.

The present wave of bubbly faith in Jesus and Christian witnessing has an element about it that causes some question. Such witnessing seems to insist that if you will accept Jesus, all your troubles will vanish and everything will come up roses. Some almost promise health, wealth, and wisdom—zing!—just like that. But it does not truly picture faith in God. Next to the resurrected Lazarus, we must put the beheaded John the Baptist. Next to Enoch we must put the stoned-to-death Stephen. Next to the translated Elijah we must place the crucified Peter. Faith is not a life insurance policy.

The problem seems to come from a claim to have here and now the joy, peace, glory, security, perfect health, and infinite knowledge of the hereafter. Now, undoubtedly God blesses His saints and bestows on them the gifts of the Spirit. But we dare not forget the knife in the hand of the Vinedresser, lest those who find their unwarranted expectations unfulfilled will give up faith altogether.

The war against sin is not over. We still live in the flesh. God has not yet destroyed the devil and his supporters. Our inherited and cultivated tendencies to evil still clamor for attention, always waiting to dominate our lives. We cannot lay off the armor of our warfare for one moment, because we have an unsleeping and relentless foe. Although He who keeps Israel does not slumber or sleep and although they that be with us are more than they that be with them, the gates of pearl have not yet swung open to us. It is nearly time. The best —preceded by the worst—is just ahead. There is still room to doubt and still evidence enough to believe. We can still make our choice every day, every hour, and every moment until He comes.

Of course, there is a sense in which heaven begins *now,* and we would not leave that out of the picture. "As through Jesus we enter into rest, heaven begins here. We respond to His invitation, Come, learn of Me, and in thus coming we begin the life eternal. Heaven is a ceaseless approaching to God through Christ. The longer we are in the heaven of bliss, the more and still more of glory will be opened to us; and the more we know of God, the more intense will be our happiness. As we walk with Jesus in this life, we may be filled with His love, satisfied with His presence. All that human nature can bear, we may receive here. But what is this compared with the hereafter?'' (*The Desire of Ages,* pp. 331, 332).

So we come to the counsel of the apostle: ''Take care, brethren, lest there be in any of you an evil, unbelieving heart, leading you to fall away from the living God. But exhort one another every day, as long as it is called 'today,' that none of you may be hardened by the deceitfulness of sin. For we share in Christ, if only we hold our first confidence firm to the end'' (Hebrews 3:12-14, RSV).

What shall we do while we wait to communicate with God face-to-face? ''Since then we have a great high priest who has passed through the heavens, Jesus, the Son of God, let us hold fast our confession. For we have not a high priest who is unable to sympathize with our weaknesses, but one who in every respect has been tempted as we are, yet without sinning. Let us then with confidence draw near to the throne of grace, that we may receive mercy and find grace to help in time of need'' (Hebrews 4:14-16, RSV).

We have no adequate idea what these times of need will be. Ellen G. White has warned that while trouble is often worse in anticipation than in realization, this will not be true of the final tribulation (see *The Great Controversy,* p. 622). But God has given a prescription to those who will face the coming troubles. Perhaps we have heard the prescription so often that we do not consider it adequate. Or we may assume that our familiarity with the prescription means that we are already taking the divine medicine. May we see once again for what the Lord would prepare us and the means He would use.

''None but those who have fortified the mind with the truths of the Bible will stand through the last great conflict'' (*ibid.,* p. 593).

''The fearful judgments denounced against the worship of the beast and his image . . . should lead all to a diligent study of the prophecies to learn what the mark of the beast is, and how they are to avoid receiving it'' (*ibid.,* p. 594).

''An understanding of Bible truth depends not so much on the power of intellect brought to the search as on the singleness of purpose, the earnest longing after righteousness'' (*ibid.,* p. 599).

''As the time comes for . . . [the message of the third angel] to be given with greatest power, the Lord will work through humble instruments. . . . Men of faith and prayer will be constrained to go forth with holy zeal, declaring the words thich God gives them'' (*ibid.,* p. 606).

''The words of Paul will be literally fulfilled, 'All that will live godly in Christ Jesus shall suffer persecution' '' (*ibid.,* p. 608).

''As the 'former rain' was given, in the outpouring of the Holy Spirit at the opening of the gospel, to cause the upspringing of the precious seed, so the 'latter rain' will be given at its close for the ripening of the harvest'' (*ibid.,* p. 611).

''Here are 'the times of refreshing' to which the apostle Peter looked forward when he said: 'Repent ye therefore, and be converted, that your sins may be blotted out, when the times of refreshing shall come from the presence of the Lord; and He shall send Jesus.' Acts 3:19, 20'' (*ibid.,* p. 612).

''By thousands of voices, all over the earth, the warning will be given. Miracles will be wrought, the sick will be healed, and signs and wonders will follow the believers. Satan also works with lying wonders, even bringing down fire from heaven in the sight of men. Revelation 13:13. Thus the inhabitants of the earth will be brought to take their stand'' *(ibid.)*

''When the third angel's message closes, mercy no longer pleads for the guilty inhabitants of the earth. The people of God have accomplished their work. They have received 'the latter rain,' 'the refreshing from the presence of the Lord,' and they are prepared for the trying hour before them. Angels are hastening to and fro in heaven. An angel returning from the earth announces that his work is done; the final test has been brought upon the world, and all who have proved themselves loyal to the divine precepts have received 'the seal of the living God' '' (*ibid.,* p. 613).

''Then Jesus ceases His intercession in the sanctuary above. . . . Every case has been decided for life or death. Christ has made the atonement for His people and blotted out their sins. The number of His subjects is made up'' (*ibid.,* pp. 613, 614).

''Satan will then plunge the inhabitants of the earth into one great, final trouble'' (*ibid.,* p. 614).

''The people of God will then be plunged into those scenes of affliction and distress described by the prophet as the time of Jacob's trouble. 'Thus saith the Lord: We have heard a voice of trembling, of fear, and not of peace. . . . All faces are turned into paleness. Alas!

for that day is great, so that none is like it: it is even the time of Jacob's trouble' " (*ibid.,* p. 616).

"As Satan accuses the people of God on account of their sins, the Lord permits him to try them to the uttermost" (*ibid.,* p. 618).

"Those who delay a preparation for the day of God cannot obtain it in the time of trouble or at any subsequent time. The case of all such is hopeless" (*ibid.,* p. 620).

"God's love for His children during the period of their severest trial is as strong and tender as in the days of their sunniest prosperity; but it is needful for them to be placed in the furnace of fire; their earthliness must be consumed, that the image of Christ may be perfectly reflected" (*ibid.,* p. 621).

"All who will lay hold of God's promises, as . . . [Jacob] did, and be as earnest and persevering as he was, will succeed as he succeeded" *(ibid.)*

"Those who exercise but little faith now, are in the greatest danger of falling under the power of satanic delusions and the decree to compel the conscience. And even if they endure the test they will be plunged into deeper distress and anguish in the time of trouble, because they have never made it a habit to trust in God" (*ibid.,* p. 622).

"We should *now* acquaint ourselves with God by proving His promises. Angels record every prayer that is earnest and sincere. We should rather dispense with selfish gratifications than neglect communion with God. The deepest poverty, the greatest self-denial, with His approval, is better than riches, honors, ease, and friendship without it. We *must* take time to pray" (*ibid.,* italics supplied).

"*Now,* while our great High Priest is making the atonement for us, we should seek to become perfect in Christ. Not even by a thought could our Saviour be brought to yield to the power of temptation" (*ibid.,* p. 623, italics supplied).

"It is in this life that we are to separate sin from us, through faith in the atoning blood of Christ. Our precious Saviour invites us to join ourselves to Him, to unite our weakness to His strength, our ignorance to His wisdom, our unworthiness to His merits" *(ibid.).*

"It rests with us to co-operate with the agencies which Heaven employs in the work of conforming our characters to the divine model" *(ibid.).*

An unbelievably glorious destiny awaits those who triumph over the beast, his image, and his mark. Not all of God's present-day children, however, will pass through the final trials. Many will sleep in Jesus before then. But the great question now is, "Am I abiding in the vine today?" Then whether we sleep in Jesus or are preserved without seeing death, we can trust Him in whom we abide. We shall bear fruit to the Father's glory for all eternity.

Whether we sleep or whether we live through the time of Jacob's trouble, we shall see His face. "All who have died in the faith of the third angel's message come forth from the tomb glorified, to hear God's covenant of peace with those who have kept His law" (*ibid.*, p. 637).

Then we will resume our eternal education. We will receive the face-to-face revelations of God that sin postponed in Eden. Every unselfish interest that we could conceive, fields of knowledge scarcely contemplated, every question in the long controversy between good and evil, every soul-longing ever felt—all will be met with unlimited resources and unlimited time when God will speak with us face-to-face.

God is there. He has spoken!

For Additional Reading

Since the North American Bible Conference of 1974 concentrated on the basis for confidence in the authority of the Bible and on the principles for its interpretation, both the *Symposium on Biblical Hermeneutics,* which was sent to delegates in advance, and a number of the Bible Conference papers themselves offer helpful reading on the main theme of this book. Also, from the wealth of materials being published by evangelical authors and others, a number would prove particularly helpful:

Berkouwer, G. C. *General Revelation*. Studies in Dogmatics. Grand Rapids: Wm. B. Eerdmans Publishing Company, 1955.

Cauthen, Kenneth. *The Impact of American Religious Liberalism*. New York: Harper & Row, Publishers, 1962.

Coleman, Richard J. *Issues of Theological Warfare: Evangelicals and Liberals*. Grand Rapids: Wm. B. Eerdmans Publishing Company, 1972.

General Conference of Seventh-day Adventists. *North American Bible Conference 1974*. Produced by the Biblical Research Committee of the General Conference of Seventh-day Adventists. Washington, D.C.: General Conference of SDA, 1974.

Hamilton, Kenneth. *Revolt Against Heaven*. Grand Rapids: Wm. B. Eerdmans Publishing Company, 1965.

Hasel, Gerhard F. *Old Testament Theology: Basic Issues in the Current Debate*. Grand Rapids: Wm. B. Eerdmans Publishing Company, 1972.

Henry, Carl F. H., ed. *Revelation and the Bible*. Grand Rapids: Baker Book House, 1969.

Hordern, William. Introduction, Vol. I: *New Directions in Theology Today*. Philadelphia: The Westminster Press, 1966.

Hyde, Gordon M., ed. *A Symposium on Biblical Hermeneutics*. Washington, D.C.: General Conference of SDA, 1974.

Ladd, George Eldon. *The New Testament and Criticism*. Grand Rapids: Wm. B. Eerdmans Publishing Company, 1967.

Machen, J. Gresham. *Christianity and Liberalism*. Grand Rapids: Wm. B. Eerdmans Publishing Company, 1972.

Mickelsen, Berkeley A. *Interpreting the Bible*. Grand Rapids: Wm. B. Eerdmans Publishing Company, 1970.

Pache, Rene. *The Inspiration and Authority of Scripture*. Chicago: Moody Press, 1969.

Ramm, Bernard L. *Hermeneutics*. Practical Theology Series. Grand Rapids: Baker Book House, 1967.

__________. *The Pattern of Religious Authority*. Grand Rapids: Wm. B. Eerdmans Publishing Company, 1968.

__________. *Special Revelation and the Word of God*. Grand Rapids: Wm. B. Eerdmans Publishing Company, 1968.

Rudnick, Miltin L. *Fundamentalism and the Missouri Synod*. St. Louis: Concordia Publishing House, 1966.